The Invisible Architect's Life-Saving Message...

"There's something not quite right with Barb's flight from Dulles to LAX—change the date!"

This is one of the most incredible *inner voice* life-and-death communications that I have ever received, and I am glad I acted on it! After my first wife passed, I was contacted by my high school sweetheart, Barbara Simpson, as she saw me on the Internet and wanted to say hello. I hadn't seen her for over thirty-eight years and always wondered what had happened to her. She didn't know I had just lost my wife a year earlier, but as we began catching up on the phone, the discussion quickly evolved into a refreshing new relationship for both of us, a relationship I had not been looking for as I was still in mourning.

A few months later, I invited her to my home in Los Angeles. So, she booked a flight on a Tuesday a few weeks later in 2001, a year and nine months after my late wife passed from an aggressive breast cancer. A couple of weeks before her flight, I got a strong *inner voice* communication to change her flight without an explanation. I called her and told her to change her flight, and she kept asking me why. I said, "Just trust me and do it, as I sense something is not quite right." She thought I was getting cold feet about seeing her. Anyway, she did change her flight, and if you haven't guessed it, that was 9/11 and her flight was number seventy-seven from Dulles, one of the hijacked planes that went into the Pentagon. She changed her flight to three days later, and the rest was history.

Imagine what would've happened had I not followed my *Invisible Architect*'s advice. Now if that wasn't a sign that we needed to be together forever, I don't know what would be.

We eventually got married and have been together ever since!

John & Barbara Novello

THE INVISIBLE ARCHITECT

HOW TO DESIGN
YOUR PERFECT LIFE
FROM WITHIN

JOHN NOVELLO

Paperback ISBN: 978-1-64719-219-8
Hardcover ISBN: 978-1-64719-327-0
Epub ISBN: 978-1-64719-220-4
Mobi ISBN: 978-1-64719-221-1

Published by BookLocker.com, Inc., St. Petersburg, Florida.

Printed on acid-free paper.

BookLocker.com, Inc.
2021

First Edition

Library of Congress Cataloguing in Publication Data
Novello, John
The Invisible Architect: How To Design Your Perfect Life From Within
by John Novello
Library of Congress Control Number: 2020923896

*Dedicated to my wife, Barbara Novello and to
all those desirous of a better life!*

ALSO BY JOHN NOVELLO

The Contemporary Keyboardist (1986)

The Contemporary Keyboardist for Beginners (2006)

The Contemporary Keyboardist Three-Part DVD Series (1991)

Stylistic Etudes (1996)

The Song That Never Ended (2003)

Table of Contents

FOREWORD

I take it seriously when someone asks me to read their book and write a foreword, even though I usually say no! It is not the work but the content that has to be of high standards.

But you will be pleased to know that in this case, I was so impressed by the material that I had to do what I do with classics like "Think and Grow Rich" by Napoleon Hill or the "Master Key System" by Charles Haanel—namely, I read them, put them on the shelf for several days, and don't think about the content. Then I pick the book back up and really study and meditate over each morsel and key thought.

Sidebar: I met John years ago when he registered and attended "The Master Key System"—an online six-month course I delivered on *mindset and manifestation* principles. It was a very tough time for John emotionally due to deaths in his family and his music career not moving in the direction he wanted, but he was determined to complete it, which he did!

I will let John share his side of the story, but I will tell you this: It would not have been possible for me to work through this demanding online course had I had John's burden. John, for years, has validated his hero status with me!

So, I read the first few chapters and told John I would be honored to write the foreword. Then I got lost in his magnificent work!

So, here is my advice…

1. Slow down, savor, and stop from time to time and think about what you are reading. To help you in this endeavor, pay attention to the questions at the end of each chapter, which John refers to as "cognitions." Why? Because these cognitions are valuable life-realizations to be applied. Because, you see, John discovered the doorway to a life second to none…the world of metaphysics.

2. Apply. If you apply what you are learning in this instant classic, you'll begin surprising yourself. You'll start seeing inexplicable things happen in your favor, and your heart will soar!

I'm excited for you, and so I've jumped a tad ahead. It's not really what we read but what we learn and apply from what we read. One of the best attributes in John's book is the introduction to *The Invisible Architect*. Who is it? Where is it? What is it? And more importantly, how can you use it to help you design a better outcome for your life?

Once you discover the *Invisible Architect* and can hear its voice, your life will never be the same. Wonder, joy, and bliss beckon you, and kindred spirits are impelled toward you magically!

Sound extreme? Too much hype? I get it, I really do. When I first tapped the world of metaphysics back in the mid-'90s, I could not believe it either. Weird and wonderful—so weird and wonderful, you might feel gloriously strange!

Let's face it…we all know how unfair it is for a child to die before the parent. So, on top of this challenging, impossibly difficult course, John's daughter got ill and eventually passed. (Note: His wife had passed away twenty years earlier from the same illness!)

Now just to sweeten the pot here, John is a wonderful, successful, critically acclaimed musician, but he had never been up front per his ambition.

He performed with great musicians all his life but never developed his solo career as he desired and deserved. Then, as you will read in the book, he found the *Invisible Architect* and heard the whispering of his heart, all while coping with his burdens. How he managed to give the course its due diligence I'll never know, but he did it and with excellence!

So now what happens? He finishes the course and shortly thereafter hits number one on Billboard as a solo performer!

As John writes, "Like most of us, I had no focused plan on how to achieve or manifest anything. All I knew was that I loved music and its positive effect on me and others. I just wanted—desired—to be a good musician and play in a band."

So how does that sort of humble statement about his music—true but not the whole truth—impact him? How does he overcome all that and really begin to express the wonder of himself?

If you are reading this in the hopes of discovering the answer as to whether you should buy this book or not…I will take a risk here and make it easy for you.

There are no common people; there is greatness within all of us. We each have some gift, skill, voice, and words to help others…an endless list, really. So, here is the risk. I will either make it easy for you to put this book down or to buy it and commit to really doing it.

Do you have thoughts that you could have more, be more, and be happy? Are you a bit sad, or mad, or angry, or frustrated that you are not happy? Do you use the underperformance of your friends with their lives to justify your own? If any of this sounds like you, buy the book. If you bought it but haven't started reading and applying…giddy-up! You are holding the key to the vault!

Me? I went from bankrupt to beachfront, living the dream on Kauai, Hawaii, for the past ten years.

Q: How'd it happen for me?

A: Surrender!!!

You see, before the criteria to maximize this book in your life (1. Slow down and 2. Apply), you've got to nail the qualifier: honesty!

What do you genuinely want? Like most people I know you have a list of what you don't want (credit card debts, bills, mortgage or rent, etc.). But what do you really want? Your heart already knows, and I'm not being "sappy" here. More messages are passed from heart to mind than mind to the entire body!

Know what yours is telling you? Do you really want to die with that magnificent dream and song in your heart unmanifested and unplanned?

It all comes down to understanding that we are spiritual beings who occasionally have human experiences. We can virtually manifest on demand if what we are seeking is good for us and others and if it is derived via service.

So, what stops us? We have been conditioned to fit in, to be average. Again, there are no average people, no common people. As a result of the conditioning and being mired in the momentum of mediocrity for decades, we've not only forgotten we are sons and daughters of the Spiritual King, but we also don't hear the voice of our own divinity anymore.

Why? Our spiritual mechanics need repair. John defines that this way: "the relationship between the Universal Energy (the *Invisible Architect*) and its creations and the interactions thereof."

The real challenge is that most of us are unfamiliar with this flawless mechanism between our ears. Meaning? We've got the greatest mechanism on the planet, our mind, but we are inexperienced or poor operators of this most remarkable gift.

Get honest and think about a perfect world. Both John and I and thousands of others are proof it is never too late to find the song of your heart and manifest its dreams. Get honest: Imagine all your bills are gone, house paid, an abundance of income coming in monthly, and you're progressing to your dreams…What would you do?

Read, study, and apply. And when you do, with John's help, open-mindedness, and work, you can stun yourself repetitiously!

Keep giving to keep growing—believe!

Mark Januszewski

Why This Book?

Angel number[1] 1111 symbolizes that the universe has opened an energy gateway for you. The universe has recognized you and is reaching out to you to help. It is a message from your angels to be very aware of your persistent thoughts and ideas as these are manifesting rapidly into your reality.[2] That's why you're reading this book!

—*John Novello*

Somewhere, in the future—if there is such a thing—your ideal Divine self and life await manifestation. Your journey may be long, but so long as you believe in angels, you will never walk alone for long.

I remember how excited I was about the future and its challenges way back when I left my home in Erie, Pennsylvania, to start my personal lifestyle journey, one I didn't even fully understand I was on.

Like most of us, I had no focused plan on how to achieve or manifest anything. All I knew was that I loved music and its positive effect on me and others. I just wanted—desired—to be a good musician and play in a

---

[1] Angel numbers work in accordance with the tenets of numerology, which upholds the notion that each number is connected to a certain vibrational energy or frequency that encompasses meaning beyond its sheer numeric value.

[2] Joanne Walmsley, Sacred Scribes Australia, sacredscribes@gmail.com

band. I didn't realize that desire was a seed I had planted in my subconscious garden, my subjective mind, awaiting objectified expression in the garden of reality. That desire began driving me forward. I listened to great musicians and looked for the best music teachers and schools. Yes, that was a plan of sorts, but I had no knowledge of what I now refer to as the Thought or Mental Universe, one's inner world or subconscious, where all creative manifestations occur. I had no knowledge or understanding of our personal spiritual architect, the Invisible Power, which all of us have at our disposal to create a better life, if only we understand its three fundamentals:

1. A higher "invisible" force or universal energy is responsible for and permeates everything. Therefore, it is everything! It makes no difference whether you believe all things were created by an all-encompassing, transcendent god or a distinct personal god, anthropomorphic or otherwise.

2. This higher force or energy is available to help us manifest our desires once we understand its spiritual mechanics. It is sometimes referred to as your inner voice, higher self, instinct, intuition, or gut feeling.

3. We are, in fact, always using this energy but not efficiently, due to our lack of knowledge regarding its mechanics.

"I of myself can do nothing; the Father within me He doeth the work."

–Neville Goddard, Biblical paraphrase

The first time I heard this quote I was a teenager studying catechism. I didn't really understand it then, but I do now. I didn't know that by improving the quality and focus of my individual thoughts and beliefs, correct decisions and actions would amplify and invite the invisible power available to all of us to express itself through me and help me design my life. In other words, I didn't understand that focusing my attention on my outer-world desires and little to none on the design of my inner-world desires was backwards.

Therefore, my biggest revelation, which seems silly in hindsight, was that to get rid of any unwanted life condition, all I needed to do was change what was causing that unwanted condition! Why fuss directly with the unwanted condition? Focus on the thought, belief, or attitude that is the cause creating the effect. Then the unwanted condition begins transforming almost magically to the new condition given the new cause. Some refer to this as simply changing one's mindset or point of view. How quickly this manifestation occurs is directly proportional to your effective use of this *invisible power* available to us all.

But who or what is helping us achieve our desires?

Are we alone in this macrocosm, or are we our own microcosm—a harmonic individual of the Universal Energy, the *Invisible Architect*—and, as such, do we co-create and design our lives through our thoughts, beliefs, and desires? I believe this is so, given my incredible interactions with the *Invisible Architect,* which I'm excited to share with you. So, please, read on!

"Life is that quality or principle of the Universal Energy which manifests in so-called organic objects as growth and voluntary activity, and which is usually co-existent in some degree, with some manifestation of that same Universal Energy as the quality or principle termed intelligence."

—Charles Haanel

Have you ever noticed that the beginning of any desire starts with a thought, a cause. Then and only then is it possible to create the desire or effect. (Think about this for a minute.) Have you ever had a desire not preceded by a thought? Look around you and try finding something that doesn't have a thought behind it—a car, computer, a skyscraper, an argument, a flower, or even the universe for that matter! Effects don't seem to just appear out of thin air; they are caused!

"Once you make a decision, the universe conspires to make it happen..."

—Ralph Waldo Emerson

Cognition: The mental action or process of acquiring knowledge and understanding through thought, experience, and the senses; cognitive mental processes; enlightenment; insight; awareness.

But why would a jazz musician write such a book? For that matter, what even qualifies me to do so?

I'm not a philosopher, theosophist, mystic, physicist, or even a well-known success author or motivational speaker—at least not yet!

Answer: To achieve any one of my desires, I really had to work at it. It did not come easy. I watched my hard-working parents struggle, as well as many of my friends. But my strong urge to achieve my desires drove me to an obsessive study of personal growth and development that included religious and philosophic studies, theosophy, mathematics, logic, and ethics. I wanted to know my nature and the nature of my interaction with the world into which I was born.

This all came into better focus after my late wife's passing in January 2000. Why? Because this was such a traumatic incident for me—the loss of my soul mate after a horrific fight with cancer—that my obsessive study of philosophy and theosophy mentioned above accelerated and led me into the field of ADCs—after death communications! In one year, I literally researched and read almost a hundred books covering the afterlife, ADCs, OBEs (out of body experiences), the Law of Attraction, New Thought, Quantum Spirituality, Soul transformation, Spiritual development, and more. I even contacted famous mediums and psychics and had many successful sessions where my late wife came through. This study and research led to my writing an earlier book called *The Song That Never Ended*.

Now I would like to share the cognitions that occurred during my journey. I sincerely hope they help you on yours!

—John Novello

Cognition 1
The Invisible Architect

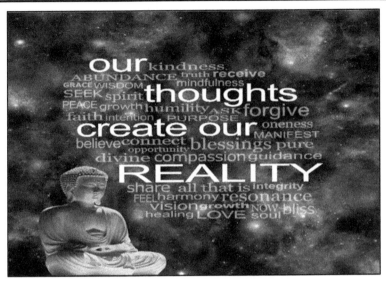

"*Mental action is the interaction of the individual upon the Universal Mind, and as the Universal Mind is the intelligence which pervades all space and animates all living things, this mental action and reaction is the Law of Causation.*"–Charles Haanel, *Mental Chemistry*

Early in my life I realized I was not alone. Indeed, I had the ultimate best friend, bodyguard, counselor, consultant, assistant, and personal life architect ever!

Who, you may ask?

This companion has been known by many names—God[3], the Universal Mind, First Cause, the Infinite Intelligence, Hidden Power, the Absolute, the Silence, the Intelligent Quantum Energy Field, the Changeless, the

---

[3]The incorporeal divine Principle ruling over all as eternal Spirit: infinite Mind, Merriam-Webster.

Ageless, the Almighty Creator, One Great Light, Universal Energy, the One, the Force, Higher Self, Intuition etc.—the *Invisible Architect*![4]

The *Invisible Architect*—those individual terms are worth defining:

Invisible: 1. unable to be seen; not visible; concealed from sight; hidden; treated as if unable to be seen; 2. ignored or not taken into consideration.

Architect: 1. a person who designs buildings and, in many cases, also supervises their construction; 2. a person who is responsible for inventing or realizing an idea or project.

The second definition applies here.

Some personal thoughts about creation (not meant to infringe on anybody's beliefs):

What are the odds that this universe created itself—whether by some sort of gradient evolution or by a big bang? The complexity, exact laws, and constants of the universe that physicists have discovered so far—I don't doubt there are many more undiscovered—that had to be put in place, let alone stay in perfect equilibrium, for harmonious existence and operation, are beyond human in nature! Changing any one of them even a little can have extreme consequences!

Did you ever look at a skyscraper, a personal computer, a space shuttle, a Ferrari, a cell phone, a software program (I could go on and on), and think they created themselves? Did you think any one of them just self-manifested without any thought, designer, or creator? How about the

---

[4]Note: From time to time, I will refer to the *Invisible Architect* using one of the other identities mentioned above. This is done to ensure better understanding given the different beliefs and different names associated with the Almighty Creator.

miracle of life? Could it have created itself in all its abundant forms—atoms, cells, tissues, organs, organisms?

Then consider the miracle of the human body. Humans, at the time of this writing, number 7.7 billion, each of us being unique! And we share this planet with as many as 8.7 million different forms of life, all with unique designs and urges to survive. Did the human body create itself? You may say it's simple biology. The sperm impregnates the ovum, and we get life. That further proves my point. Who or what created the blueprint that created the process that evolves into life?[5] Was evolution created as a tool in the process of creation?

Does a book write itself? Does a song compose and record itself? Does a computer's operating system software write itself, let alone a computer's hardware create itself?

What are the odds of a pile of iron, wires, electronics, circuit boards, rubber, and plastic falling over and becoming a Bentley, or a Honda, or anything but a fallen-down chaotic rearrangement of iron, wires, rubber, circuit boards, and plastic?

Answer: Zero! "Something" had to put this universe together. Right?

Just as it takes human intelligence and skill to create, don't we have to believe there is some intelligence who created us?

From logical reasoning, empirical evidence, and my own personal experience, there appears to be an *Ordering Intelligence*, an Architect, somewhere in this life equation—an ether, a theoretical energy substance, a quantum field—that permeates and connects all and thus

---

[5]Evolution does not explain the origin of life, but how it developed after it appeared on earth. ... In other words, to have evolution there needs to be a pre-existing gene pool, meaning life already must exist. Some theories attempt to explain the origin of life, notably including the abiogenesis theory. Yes, a giraffe gets taller through natural selection, but how did eyeballs suddenly appear? How did two organisms of the same species develop sex organs that perfectly mated with the opposite gender? Darwin, and no one, has answers for these questions.

acts as a medium for both physical and spiritual communication and interaction.

Is it possible that this energy substance is intelligent, responds to our thoughts, and shapes our desires?

Why not?

The more I contemplated my relationship with this energy substance, I became more and more aware not only of its nature but also of its willingness to assist me in designing and achieving my life urges, urges that I knew I had a duty to achieve.

At first, I didn't understand. But through personal study and miraculous experiences, I have learned that we are all unique, creative thoughts (manifestations) of *The One* who seeks expression through each of us, contingent on our awareness, understanding, and personal invitation to do so.

This is so important that I will state it again: *We are all unique, creative manifestations—thoughts—of The One who seeks expression through each of us, contingent on our awareness, understanding, and personal invitation to do so.*

This truth leads to the next question: If indeed there is this Intelligent Universal Energy, what is its nature, purpose, and relationship to you and me? What are the spiritual mechanics?

How does this work?

Q&A Cognition 1

1. Q: Who or what is the *Invisible Architect*?
   A: An Intelligent Universal Energy that created and animates all things and which seeks expression through each of us contingent to our awareness, understanding, and personal invitation to do so; the Universal Mind; God.

2. Q: Is it logical to assume the universe just evolved somehow by chance on its own?
   A: Unlikely, given its complexity, exact laws, and constants that physicists have discovered that had to be put in place, let alone stay in perfect equilibrium for harmonious existence!

3. Have you ever thought you were not alone, that there was a higher energy or intelligence? If so, try recalling when and what you were doing at the time and write it down or review it in your mind! If not, read on…

4. Q: Are each of us creations of the *Invisible Architect* or just random accidents of nature?
   A: We are each unique, creative thoughts (manifestations) of The One who seeks expression through each of us contingent to our awareness, understanding, and personal invitation to do so.

5. If you have experience with the *Invisible Architect,* what names do you use to refer to this phenomenon?

Next Cognition…

Cognition 2
Awareness of the Architect
(My Inner Voice)

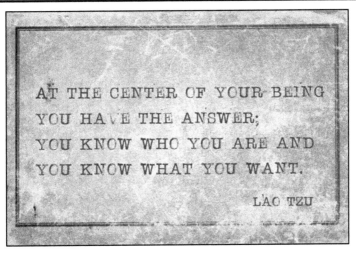

"*At the center of your being, you have the answer; you know who you are, and you know what you want.*"

–Lao Tzu

"*He must consciously commune with the Indwelling Power and Presence, and receive guidance, strength, vitality, and all things necessary for the fulfillment of his needs.*"

–Joseph Murphy

I became aware of the *Invisible Architect* (though at the time I did not know it by that name) when I was around three years old. At that time, I referred to the Architect as my "inner voice." At that pivotal moment, I became aware that my life seemed guided, or that I had some special intuition or precognitive abilities.

At the time, I thought everybody had this inner voice or guide, and although I was right, most were so involved with life's challenges that they either weren't paying attention, or they were simply ignoring their all-knowing advisor—they didn't know they had it!

The first time my inner voice came to me, I was watching *The Lawrence Walk Show*. This was in Erie, Pennsylvania, where I was born and grew up, a small all-American hamburger town—hardly a city known for the arts. I was sitting in front of the TV, watching the famous Dick Contino play the accordion. A clear inner voice said: *That's it! Point to it now!*

I immediately pointed to the accordion on the TV screen. My mother, Menga, short for Domenica (of Italian origin, meaning "belonging to the Lord") took this to mean that I wanted to play the accordion. (Bless her sweet soul, as she now is with the Lord.) She was almost correct as, yes, I wanted to play, but not the accordion. What I really wanted to do was play the piano. But at three years old, I wasn't quite articulate enough to make the distinction. All I knew was that my *inner voice* had been directing me to point to those black and white keys!

From then on, every time this inner voice spoke, I listened! Sometimes, my new friend told me to do something, sometimes not to do something. I also eventually realized I could ask this all-knowing source for advice, and if I paid attention, the answer would be forthcoming—in fact, not only forthcoming, but immediately present and clear.

I have had countless *inner voice* consultations over the years, and these "gut feelings" continue to this day—they're amazing! Some of the guidance is even miraculous, as you shall soon see. Below is a chronological account of some of my key real-life interactions with this Divine, all-knowing, all-caring consultant. Some of the interactions give career advice, some financial advice; some are informational in nature due to my direct queries, some are spiritual, and some even address matters of life and death!

By sharing these stories, I hope to demonstrate not only the wondrous possibilities but also the Divine power that we all have available within. We may use this amazing power for designing our lives from within once we understand the spiritual mechanics involved. And the best thing is that this inner power is entirely free!

The format for this account is threefold: a) the topic or category; b) a statement of the advice given by my *inner voice* to some event or question; and c) an explanation of the circumstances.

And by the way, beyond what I enumerate here, there are hundreds, perhaps thousands, of *inner voice* consultations. They happen often, sometimes daily; there are so many that it would be an abnormality if they didn't occur. I've included only twenty to show you some possibilities for interaction. Although all of my *Invisible Architect* interactions have been special and fruitful, some may need additional commentary, which I will provide in the next section.

1. **The Beginning of My Music Career:** "That's it!" My inner voice is here referring to the accordion player that I saw on TV during *The Lawrence Welk Show*. This guidance led my parents to start me on accordion lessons when I was nine years old, which opened the door to my incredible music career!

2. **Career Advice:** "Piano, not the accordion." The inner voice is referring to a change of musical instruments. I was to give up the accordion at the age of thirteen and switch to the piano and organ. Apparently, it was my destiny as a musician to play these instruments instead.

3. **The Nature of Reality:** "Yes, outer space is infinite, and you are, too." The inner voice speaks here in response to my query about outer space being endless. This important message from the Architect about my eternal existence eventually led me back to my spiritual roots. (For more on this topic, see my discussion in the next section.)

4. **Career Encouragement:** "You can do that." Here, the inner voice is validating that I could have my own band, which would be just as successful as the bands on TV. I thought, *Yeah, I want to do that.* Shortly afterward, some local musicians asked me to join their band, which started my commercial music career. I was beginning to get the knack at manifesting my desires through my thoughts and strong beliefs!

5. **Career Direction:** "This is not the right direction." The inner voice is here referring to the option of an academic career. I had

been considering a Ph.D. in mathematics. Instead, I agreed with my inner guidance and chose a career in music. From then on, I envisioned my success as a musician every day. Shortly thereafter, my band got discovered by a famous record producer! The producer just happened to be passing through my hometown of Erie on his way to Cleveland, Ohio. (For more on this topic, see my discussion in the next section.)

6. **The Meaning of Events:** "You were not ready for this success. For what you're destined to do in life, you need to get better trained musically and move out West." Here, the inner voice is giving me perspective on what is best to do considering my future. I had asked a question about the meaning of some apparent bad luck: "Why did my band's singer get drafted, causing Mainline Records to drop us, just when our record had been climbing the charts?" The advice from my inner guide led me to move to Boston to attend the prestigious Berklee College of Music, where I immersed myself in all aspects of music, gaining an excellent preparation for my music career in California.

7. **Advice About My Playing Goals:** "Contact the musicians who inspire you to learn more." Here the inner voice is responding to my enthusiasm about my jazz heroes: "Wow, the records by Oscar Peterson and Chick Corea that my drummer gave me blow me away! I want to be able to play like that. What's my next step?" Taking the advice of my inner guide, I figured out a way to contact and meet both jazz legends, which greatly enhanced my career progress! (For more on this topic, see my discussion in the next section.)

8. **Advice to Solve a Financial Crisis:** "Hang out at all the jazz clubs and major music stores to network." The inner voice is here answering my desperate need once I landed in LA without money or connections. "Okay, I'm out West in Los Angeles, don't know anybody, and I'm broke as hell. Now what?" I followed the advice of my inner guide, and guess what? The

keyboardist of a new band, A Taste of Honey, heard me playing at the Guitar Center in Los Angeles, where I used to go network (per the advice of my inner voice). He took my contact info, and three months later, his band's first record at Capital Records (*Get Down Boogie Oogie Oogie*) got released and sold two million. I became their musical director. By this chain of contacts and events, my money problem was solved as did other problems, since that gig opened many musical doors!

9. **Serendipity:** "Why don't you take the subway instead of the band limo?" *What?* I thought. I asked the concierge where I should go to get some authentic Japanese cuisine, and she recommended the Tokyo Wharfs, which could easily be reached by subway. (Note: Normally I would take the band limo, but my inner voice urged me to take the subway as the concierge suggested.) So, against *my* better judgment, I took a subway to the Tokyo Wharfs to get some authentic Japanese cuisine, as recommended by the hotel concierge. After lunch, I got lost and couldn't find the subway station to travel back to the hotel. I thought, *You idiot! Why didn't you take the band limo?* But then, lo and behold, a limo did come along, which got me to my destination. Note: Little did I know, but someone else very special traveled to the same area for the same reason! (For more on this topic, see my discussion in the next section.)

10. **Career Advice and Encouragement:** "Why don't *you* write the book?" The *Invisible Architect* is here coaching me to write a jazz piano instructional manual. I expressed to my inner guide my need for a book to use for piano instruction, a home business I had started in Los Angeles to earn survival income. I needed a good jazz manual that had all the music fundamentals in a single book, which would save me from having to write lessons out by hand. I could not find the kind of book I needed. After my trustworthy inner voice recommended that I write the book, I kind of pushed back, thinking, "What? I have never written a book before…But, why not?" For five years, I was consumed with the task of writing my first book, *The Contemporary*

Keyboardist, today a critically acclaimed bestseller and regarded as the Bible for contemporary keyboard instruction. Several other books and educational videos followed, elaborating on my own method in music and contemporary keyboard jazz.

11. **Career Advice:** "Don't sell your Hammond B3 organ!" The inner voice is here warning me against selling my favorite instrument to finance a move. In Erie, Pennsylvania, my place of birth, I formed a contemporary organ band called C.J. Bri, which became quite famous in the tri-state area (Pennsylvania, Ohio, and New York). My inner voice then took me out to California in 1978. I was going to sell some of my musical equipment to finance the move, but when it came to my Hammond B3, my inner voice acted up: "Don't sell your Hammond B3. You'll be needing that instrument!" (For more on this topic, see my discussion in the next section.)

12. **Medical Advice:** "Get another opinion, but I strongly suggest that you get your wife's breast tumor surgically removed, even though the diagnosis says it's benign." Here my inner voice is giving me sound medical advice, which my wife did not end up following. I passed along this information from my inner advisor to my wife at the time. But she was adamant about using diet and alternative therapies (e.g., for immune boosting) instead of the mainstream protocol (i.e., surgery, chemo, and radiation). I couldn't say that I blamed her, considering the hazards and side effects of those toxic cancer treatments. I should have been more persistent about getting another opinion. The *Invisible Architect* was right. The tumor turned out to be malignant and overly aggressive. It quickly spread to her lymph system, and after eighteen months of hell, my wife was gone!

13. **We Don't Die:** "Hey, John, everything's fine! I'm not dead...I'm here in our living room. The cancer can't hurt me anymore, as I'm free of my body. Thanks for our great life! Let's stay in touch as we promised." Here, amazingly, the Inner Architect makes possible a message from the beyond, in the

spiritual realm, as my wife is transitioning from earth. While my wife, Gloria Rusch, was dying of aggressive cancer, we as a family were praying by her side for a safe transition. Although she was still alive and breathing, her death was imminent. Her spirit was already beyond her body and inaccessible. Then suddenly, even though her body was still alive, I got that "Hey John" message as clear as if she had been standing next to me. A few minutes later, her body expired! This spiritual experience triggered my interest in the afterlife and after-death communications. As mentioned earlier, I obsessively began researching all the literature ever written about such subjects, which evolved into a book, *The Song That Never Ended*. This was my way of telling others who had lost loved ones that indeed their songs have not ended. Each of us continues singing!

14. **Life and Death Advice:** "There's something not quite right with Barb's flight from Dulles to LAX—change the date!" The inner voice here is warning me about danger. This is one of the most incredible inner voice communications, with a life-and-death urgency, that I have ever received. I am glad I acted on this guidance, as it saved the life of my wife to be. (See book's intro story.)

15. **Financial Advice:** "Don't worry about your mortgage. It's taken care of!" Here, the inner voice gives me great financial news, based on information I had not yet received. I thought, *What? Are you crazy?* I had almost gone bankrupt during the two years that my late wife and I had been fighting her cancer. I was very behind on some critical bills and worried about losing my home. A couple of months later, I received a complete "forgiveness note" of my second mortgage from Bank of America, in the amount of $186,000! At first, I thought it was a hoax, but my real estate attorney assured me otherwise: "Congratulations! You are one of one thousand or so lucky ones that they settled with for a class action suit because of all their dubious, sub-prime mortgage loans. "What a miracle, and a relief, to have my second mortgage zeroed out!

16. **Have Faith:** Here the inner voice counsels me to keep the faith. I was still facing imminent foreclosure unless I paid the past-due mortgage or negotiated a loan modification (highly unlikely). Although exceedingly difficult, my wife and I imagined our mortgage being up to date every night before we went to bed. We kept faith, having learned that nothing is impossible if you have the right viewpoint when it comes to the *Invisible Architect*. Guess what? A few weeks later my wife and I heard a home retention commercial for an attorney firm. We thought that to be a good omen, especially because we had asked the *Invisible Architect* for assistance. We called them, had an interview, and hired them on the spot. Within three weeks they had negotiated an unheard-of two percent loan modification for my first mortgage and rolled the past due into the new mortgage— problem solved! (Note: Even the home retention attorney said, "You must be blessed because we have never seen such a fast loan modification!").

17. **Dream Come True:** Here, the *Invisible Architect* behaves to me like a loving father and grants me the opportunity to get a recording studio. "Father, —I sometimes refer to the *Invisible Architect* as my spiritual father—I need to have my own recording studio to compose and record my music. To go to a professional studio is expensive, let alone inconvenient. Please help!" The sequence of events that followed were mind-blowing, and I got the studio of my dreams for free! (For more on this topic, see my discussion in the next section.)

18. **Business Advice:** "You need to help your team more." My inner advisor is here responding to my feelings of guilt over the struggles of my networking marketing group. To help the downline members to succeed, I began researching network marketing authors and courses. Through a video on list-building, an important fundamental for success, I discovered Mark Januszewski, who called himself "the world's laziest networker." Little did I know how amazing this hookup would

become! (For more on this topic, see my discussion in the next section.)

19. **Networking Advice:** "Why don't you give Andy a call?" The inner voice is here offering me a strategy for renewed musical success. While reorganizing my email contact list, I noticed the name of a good friend of mine, the *Platinum Hit* song producer Andy Goldmark. I wondered how he was doing, as I hadn't seen him for years. My *inner voice* insisted that it would be beneficial for both of us to get back together. So, we caught up over lunch. We have now produced several CDs and four top-ten hit singles on the Billboard smooth jazz chart! The song "Good to Go" went to number one! My music career began exploding all over again in a new *genre*!

Discussion Section

The Nature of Reality (see #3 above)

Not too long after the *Invisible Architect* told me I was infinite, I had a vivid dream that I was flying around the neighborhood at night. It was so real I couldn't wait to go to bed every night to experience this lucid dream again! Little did I know at the time, but I was having real out-of-body experiences. One instance was the most inspirational. It was early morning and daylight (rather than nighttime), and I got up to go to the bathroom. I was still tired. So, I went back to bed. I had the idea of wanting to fly around the neighborhood, and sure enough, within a few minutes, I was doing so! I saw one of the neighbors getting into his car to go to work. When I woke up, I realized that this experience had been real because my neighbor did that exact thing every morning. I was only about eleven at the time. I continued to experience OBEs, almost at will, until I left home at twenty to pursue my music career. Due to these early experiences, I became extremely interested in spiritual development and the nature of reality. My interests led to my writing this book fifty years later. Go figure!

Career Direction (see #5 above)

The creativity of the Architect is mind-boggling! The orchestration of events by the Architect is awesome. If you recall, I was advised to pursue music instead of a Ph.D. in mathematics. By envisioning a successful music career, I attracted a famous record producer at one of my gigs! This happened by using the Law of Attraction, which I knew nothing about at the time. A big snowstorm forced this producer to get off the I-90 freeway as he was passing through Erie on his way to Cleveland. After he checked into his room at the Ramada Inn, where my band was performing, he came down to the bar to chill from his long drive. He got a drink and listened to the music. After our set, he came up to me. He said that although he had been tired and was about to go to sleep, something had told him to go down to the bar and listen to the band. He was a producer and songwriter who really liked what he had heard.

A few weeks later, we were contacted by Mainline Records, his record label, an affiliate of MGM Records. We were offered a major record deal. A few months later, our first single, "You Won't Get Me Working," was released and quickly climbed to No. 7 on the Pop Chart. Just like that, we were on our way! Now, did this string of events happen by pure luck? Or instead by a higher power, who was orchestrating my destiny as per my desire? Whichever is the case, my fortune served as major validation that I had made the right decision in choosing music over math! Little did I know at the time, but I was employing both the *Invisible Architect* and the Law of Cause and Effect.

Advice on My Playing Goals (see #7 above)

I took the Architect's advice and traveled to Rochester, New York, about 150 miles from my hometown, to see Oscar Peterson perform. On a break, he was smoking a cigarette in the back lobby. So as not to miss the opportunity, I introduced myself as a pianist and student of jazz. He reached out to shake my hand and saw I was startled! I said, "Wow, your hand is so big, which explains why you're able to play stride piano[6] so effortlessly." His response was incredible, and in hindsight, a great piano lesson! He told me not to regret that I had been given small hands because Chopin had small hands, and look what he accomplished. He said small hands can do certain things that big hands cannot and vice versa. So, learn how to use what God gave you! This advice was validating and incredible. I never forgot it. Later in my career I gravitated toward playing the organ, for which my smaller hands became an asset, not a liability!

I also wrote a letter to jazz pianist Chick Corea at his fan-mail address. To my amazement, he responded! We began developing a great pen-pal relationship, which later led to my working with him in many capacities. I played on one of his CDs, helped program his synthesizers, and became an educational consultant for his music educational videos. He also wrote the foreword for my best-selling and critically acclaimed music instruction manual, *The Contemporary Keyboardist*, published by Hal Leonard. Later my legendary fusion band Niacin, featuring Dennis Chambers and Billy Sheehan, signed a record deal on Chick Corea's record label, Stretch Records. All of these exciting collaborations happened thanks to the *Invisible Architect*, who advised me through my inner voice. My spiritual relationship with the Architect is indeed exciting, not to mention fruitful!

Serendipity(see #9 above)

By the time I left the Japanese restaurant in an old neighborhood, it was just getting dark. I had no idea where the subway was. I was lost! So, I thought, *You should have taken the band limo instead of the subway, you idiot!* I could see the downtown Tokyo skyscrapers in the distance about ten miles away. But that was a long way to walk! There were no taxis in the neighborhood, nor could I speak Japanese. But I figured I'd at least head in the direction of the city. I expected that my inner voice and higher

---

[6]Stride is a style of jazz *piano* playing, in which the right hand plays the melody while the left hand plays a single bass note or octave, on the strong beat, and a chord on the weak beat. This style was developed in Harlem during the 1920s, partly from ragtime *piano* playing.

self, whom I had grown to trust by now, would solve my problem. So, I *imagined* being in the limo as I should have been. (Note: Here is another example of the power of the imagination for manifestation.)

Five minutes later (I kid you not), I heard a female voice. "Hey mister, what are you doing way down here? Are you lost? Do you need a ride?" I turned toward the friendly voice and saw a big, black stretch limo. This limo wasn't our band limo, and so I was a bit confused. The back window was rolled down, and the female voice belonged to Donna Summer (rest her soul). I had never met her, but she was in Tokyo to play at the famous Budokan Arena. I was there, too, to play with my band, A Taste of Honey. She had seen me rehearsing during the day and recognized me. Now what are the odds that this meeting was merely a chance occurrence in a city as large as Tokyo? A little serendipity, to say the least! I smiled, of course, and thanked my inner voice mentally. I took Donna up on the ride. Donna and I got to know each other quite well during the long ride back to the hotel, so much so that the following year she asked me to join her band, playing keyboards!

Career Advice(see #11 above)

I thought it was quite curious when my inner voice insisted, "Don't sell your Hammond B3! You'll be needing that instrument." The Hammond B3 had once been very popular and a featured sound with many rock and soul bands, such as Santana, Tower of Power, Vanilla Fudge, the Young Rascals, Jimmy Smith, Emerson, Lake & Palmer, Steppenwolf, Traffic, Yes, and many more. The instrument had been falling out of favor more recently, however. It was being replaced by the Fender Rhodes and synthesizers. Nevertheless, I trusted my inner compass, and sure enough, in 1995 legendary rock and roll bassist Billy Sheehan contacted me, as he had heard I was a good Hammond B3 player— there weren't many of us left at that time. He had always wanted to be in a band with a B3. Just like that, Niacin was born, featuring bassist Billy Sheehan, myself (on Hammond B3), and drummer extraordinaire Dennis Chambers. Niacin, as of this writing, has recorded nine CDs. We have toured the world and are considered one of the best prog rock instrumental bands of all time, so I'd say the *Invisible Architect* struck pay dirt again!

Dream Come True (See #17 above)

I have always dreamed of having my own home recording studio ready to use on my premises versus having to book a professional studio. Instead of dreaming, I closed my eyes and imagined what my life would be like owning my own home professional studio that I could work in 24/7. I envisioned being able to go compose, try things out, record them, etc. I saw other musicians coming to my studio and recording my music for me. I saw how prolific I would be and all the music I could create and distribute into the marketplace and how it would improve my career. It invigorated me to no end! I will never forget that *feeling*, as it was as real as if I already owned it and was using it. (Note: Later I discovered that *feeling* was the secret to using my *imagination* and *the Invisible Architect*'s power of manifestation. I was indeed therefore on the right track!)

After almost six months of imagining this—patience is indeed a virtue—I discovered that one of my late wife's vocal students owned a suite of recording studios, and one was available. He said I could not only use one of the professional recording suites, but I could use it for free! I thought, *Are you kidding me?* And smiled to the above! It was only ten minutes from my home! Although I had envisioned remodeling my three-car garage one day so I could have a home studio (more on this desire getting fulfilled), this sure was a step in the right direction, as a) I couldn't afford to lease a pro studio, and b) I couldn't afford the $150,000 to remodel my garage into a professional recording studio.

I of course accepted his gracious offer, and the studio was up and running in a few weeks! That was a huge manifestation and answer to my request (prayer). I composed and recorded several CD's and worked on several movies in that personal recording studio.

I was extremely happy until, one day many years later, all the studio owners in the recording complex got a letter saying the city was renovating the entire square mile of North Hollywood where my studio was located and would be using eminent domain to purchase all the buildings and land in the area.

Since we were all studio renters and not owners, the only thing the city offered was $5,000 to relocate somewhere else. That would mean finding an already existing professional recording studio or building one—both awfully expensive to do and beyond my budget at the time. I had three months to solve this major problem and move my functioning studio that I depended on for income. Weeks went by, and no answer was forthcoming from my inner voice other than "Don't worry; just believe in your original home studio dream!"

"What?" I said. I did not have the money to remodel my three-car garage and do a professional studio build-out, not even close. But then another miracle happened! A new city manager was appointed to facilitate getting all the tenants out of the building by the city's drop-dead date so they could begin demolition and construction of the new development. He met with me and asked me what my plan was and if I needed any assistance. I told him my logistical and financial predicament, and he said that there was an assistance provision of eminent domain where the city was somewhat responsible for not only relocation expenses but also for finding me a *comparable* studio.

He gave me a separate form to fill out, which was quite complicated. I noticed the section where I had to describe in detail the history of my studio suite and what it was worth and provide all supporting documents, which I did. A few weeks later, the new eminent domain agent contacted me to clarify the data. In my research, I found out that the studio complex where my studio was located was built by a famous studio designer!

In fact, the entire complex was quite famous and expensive to design—a one-of-a-kind professional studio complex with a rich history of success! The agent said that was great news if it could be validated. If so, he could submit a much higher request for not only relocation fees but for design fees, as well. As I said, the city had a "comparable clause," which stated they were responsible for finding me a similar studio and location—the *Invisible Architect* came to the rescue again! I ended up getting more than enough compensation to relocate, and guess what?

That's right…I used the income to renovate my three-car studio garage into a professional recording studio, where I composed and recorded my number one Billboard hit single "Good to Go," among many other successful musical projects…Amazing how the *Invisible Architect* orchestrated all of this!

Business Advice (See #18 above)

First, I thought that the moniker "the world's laziest networker" was brilliant, but second and more importantly, my *inner voice* said this is the one! I watched all of Mark Januszewski's free online training videos and immediately began applying his common-sense approach to network marketing, which began helping my team = income! I also attended an online network marketing "boot camp" course called "Go90Grow," which was very educational. He had built six successful network marketing companies from scratch—he was the Guru!

I soon discovered that the *Invisible Architect* was again working its magic by killing two birds with one stone. Not only was I getting the needed network marketing training for my downline, but I was also being led to the Master Key Master Mind Alliance (MKMMA), which was a six-month self-discovery course that Mark put together. This course aligned with many of the authors I was already studying how the Kingdom of God is within, and as within without; how our inner world creates our outer world; and how our thoughts create reality—the entire New Thought movement.[7] It is one thing to read and self-study spiritual development concepts but quite another to do a six-month intensive workshop with assignments, exercises, and accountability. It was life-changing and pulled the rods out of my personal nuclear inner-world reactor, thereby allowing the *Invisible Architect* to express itself through me more efficiently. It was like a controlled personal explosion of

[7]New Thought Movement – The New Thought movement is a loosely allied group of religious denominations, authors, philosophers, and individuals who share a set of beliefs concerning metaphysics, positive thinking, the Law of Attraction, healing, life force, creative visualization, and personal power. The term "New Thought" signifies that one's thoughts can unlock secrets to living a better life, free from the constraints of religious doctrines or dogmas.

Divine energy—the frosting on my personal development cake; not to mention, Mark ended up writing the foreword to this book!

There are, and there continue to be, many such miracles. They are a way of life for me. One day, I got the following, truly clear, inner voice instruction. The instruction was actually an order—very intense!

"John, you now need to spread the WORD!"

I said, "What WORD?"

"That everybody is one with the *Invisible Architect* and could be employing this miraculous energy to design their lives from within!"

"But there are already many books on this subject."

"True, but not from your unique perspective as a jazz musician who has experienced these wonderful miracles!"

And therein lies the genesis of this book! I cannot imagine operating without my mystical friend and advisor—the *Invisible Architect*. And so, it is my desire to spread the WORD to everyone!

Q&A Cognition 2

1. Q: What types of interactions are possible with the *Invisible Architect?*
   A: Some of the interactions give career advice, some financial advice. Some are informational in nature due to my direct queries, while some are spiritual. Some even address matters of life and death!

2. Q: If everybody's life interacts with and is guided by an inner voice, why do we ignore it most of the time?
   A: We are too consumed with life's challenges to pay attention. Or through lack of knowledge, we ignore it. We don't, in most cases, even know we have such an amazing spiritual friend!

3. After reading the many stories and interactions in this chapter— some of life and death significance or miraculous; others, ordinary but very useful—can you recall times when you experienced an inner voice or feeling? Some mental advice or suggestion, an intuition, hunch, dream, or coincidence? If you have experienced inner guidance in these forms, did you follow through on it? Why or why not?

4. Think about what your top three *Invisible Architect* stories would be. Why those?

5. Q: What is the WORD? What does it mean to spread the WORD?
   A: Everybody is a spiritual being and has an inner *Invisible Architect*. This Architect can be assisting them to design their ideal lives.

Next Cognition…

Cognition 3
Connecting To The Architect

"Perfect life within me, come forth into expression through me of that which I am and lead me ever into the paths of perfection causing me to see only the good; and by this process, the soul shall be illumined, acquainted with God and shall be at peace."

—*Ernest Holmes*

In his book *The Celestine Prophecy*, James Redfield states, "We have been disconnected from the larger source of dynamic universal energy that sustains us and responds to our expectations. We have cut ourselves off and so have felt weak, insecure and lacking."

I believe this statement to be accurate due to the miracles that happen and continue to happen to me, given my awareness and connection to the perfect Divine life that is in me, always awaiting manifestation! This perfect life is in all of us, awaiting our commands!

Important definitions:

Mechanics: The functional parts of an activity; the machinery or working parts of something.

Spiritual: Of the spirit or the soul as distinguished from the body or material matters.

Spiritual Mechanics: The relationship between the Universal Energy (the *Invisible Architect*) and its creations and the interactions thereof.

I have just given you many examples of interactions I have had with my inner voice—the *Invisible Architect*. I'll let you decide whether they are truly supernatural communications, coincidences, or wishful thinking.

That said, I have one hundred percent certainty that to use the inner power that I believe we are connected to—a power that I now refer to as the *Invisible Architect*—we must...

a) become aware of it,
b) learn how to consciously commune with and employ it, and
c) trust it to manifest our desires as only it knows how.

These are the spiritual mechanics that are critical to understanding how to use this power successfully because it...

a) is not only invisible but can be difficult to be conscious of, as it operates at an extremely high frequency—the God Frequency!
b) takes a certain interest and focus to communicate with and employ the power, and
c) takes faith, gratitude, and patience for the desire to be fulfilled.

Awareness of the Invisible Architect[8]

I don't claim to be an expert in this area, but I can tell you what I did that eventually helped me achieve awareness of the following:

1. There is indeed a *Perfect All-Knowing Power*, an *Invisible Architect*, or to put it in more scientific terms, an *Invisible Field of Intelligent Energy* that permeates everything that exists, including you and me and all life, matter, energy, space, and time, and is available to us for information, advice, comfort, and assistance in designing our perfect Divine lives!

---

[8]"It only requires recognition to set causes in motion which will bring about results in accordance with your desire, and this is accomplished because the Universal can act only through the individual, and the individual can act only through the Universal; they are one." —Charles Haanel

2. There are spiritual mechanics—specific ways of thinking, communicating, and interacting—necessary to utilize this power efficiently. Note: We are always using this power in a generic manner as it is innately a gift—part of the paradigm—but not very intelligently, due to our ignorance of its mechanics. In fact, we are often using this power in a self-destructive manner; more on this later.

3. Our ability to become aware of this power, develop a relationship with it, and use (apply) it ethically and constructively, is directly proportional to our spiritual growth. This growth can be consciously sped up and specialized through observation, experience, and personal knowledge to produce greater results. In fact, it is your responsibility to do so. (See Cognition 5)

4. Our relationship with the *Invisible Architect* is an individual one, for it is only through each individual that this *Intelligent Energy* can express itself through each of our desires, which is the essence of manifestation on the physical plane.

5. The *Invisible Architect* knows (expresses) itself through everyone's unique Divine gifts and developed talents, which demonstrate themselves as urges or desires. (Only man is endowed with true self-determinism, whereas other life forms appear to follow genetic blueprints versus true individual self-awareness and determinism. Nevertheless, they are expressions of the *Invisible Architect*.)

6. Each of us is therefore a *channel* or *distributor* of this power, not the *power* itself, even though we are of the same nature. If we were the power, there would be no purpose for our existence.

7. The *Invisible Architect* must be *invited* by each of us through specific spiritual mechanics to express its perfection through our unique Divine desires. Then and only then can we achieve our

full Divine expression, which ultimately is the Architect expressing itself through us. We are the channel for the expression (distribution) of the Architect's perfection manifested through us from within.[9]

8. Given that the Architect is the Supreme Source or First Cause— a Higher Intelligence; and given that the Architect is All-Knowing, All-Powerful, and All-Loving; and given we want our desires and circumstances manifested into such forms in the Physical Universe that can be expressed by the Architect, then it is imperative we not only trust the Architect to express itself through our desires, but also allow it in its own time and manner to use its powers of creativity to do so unhampered by our ignorance and limitations. Remember: We choose what we wish to experience, and the choices are unlimited!

For example, in Cognition 2, when I expressed my desire to have my own personal recording studio, I couldn't have imagined the creativity— circumstances, relationships, networking, and seeds—that were planted by the Architect to express its perfection through me to manifest my studio! In hindsight, it was and still is always a miraculous mysterious event!

Also, in Cognition 2, if you recall when I was looking up at the stars and became overwhelmed at the infinite vastness of space, I thought to myself, *Is outer space and the stars truly endless? How can that be?* The answer

---

[9]The interesting thing about this last point is the self-determinism aspect. The Merriam-Webster definition of self-determinism is "free choice of one's own acts or states without external compulsion." By allowing us the free choice to choose any desire, positive or negative, that we wish to manifest, we are given great freedom and potential to grow spiritually. We can choose imperfect livingness—ignorance, lack and scarcity, unhappiness, disease, jealousy, etc.— or we can choose perfect livingness—knowledge, love, abundance, health, happiness, etc.—the latter being the nature of the *Invisible Architect* and therefore naturally expressed.

from the Architect was, "Yes, it is as endless as you are endless." I was only nine years old at the time, but that was a spiritual moment for me, as (little did I know at the time), this began the process of making the *Invisible Architect* visible. From that moment on, I knew I was not alone. I not only had a powerful friend and ally but an *Invisible Architect* to help design my life. I became obsessed about becoming more and more knowledgeable of this *Intelligent Energy* and effectively using it for good.

But who created this game—this game we call life? The *Invisible Architect?* Or is *the Invisible Architect* a tool of another more senior Creator?

The answer to these questions would be speculation on my part, but I do know this: I have proven to myself that I can communicate with this *Intelligent Ordering Energy* for advice, for answers, and for assistance in designing my life from within.

Q&A Cognition 3

1. Q: What are spiritual mechanics and why are they important to know?
   A: Specific ways of thinking and interacting with the *Invisible Architect*; the relationship between the *Invisible Architect* and its creations and the interactions thereof.

2. Q: What must happen to be able to use our inner power—the *Invisible Architect*?
   A: We have to a) become aware of it; b) learn how to consciously commune with and employ it; and c) trust it to manifest our desires as it only knows how.

3. Q: We all have the *Invisible Architect* and its power available to us, but some are not using it very efficiently. Why?
   A: Because we are ignorant of its mechanics!

4. Q: How does the *Invisible Architect* know itself?
   A: The *Invisible Architect* knows itself by expressing itself through everyone's gifts and *developed* talents, which demonstrate themselves as urges or desires.

5. Q: What process must happen to efficiently and causatively employ the *Invisible Architect* to express itself through each of us?
   A: The Architect must be invited by each of us through specific mechanics to express its perfection through our Divine desires. (See the Be-Do-Have Formula in Cognition 5.)

6. Q: What is self-determinism?
   A: Self-determinism is the free choice of one's own acts or states of being without external compulsion. We can choose imperfection or perfection, poverty or abundance, ignorance or knowledge, disease or health, unhappiness, or happiness! (See Cognition 5 on the Be-Do-Have formula.)

7. Q: Why is it imperative to trust the *Invisible Architect?*
    A: Given the *Invisible Architect* is All-Knowing—a higher intelligence—we must allow it to express itself through our desires in its own time and manner and use its powers of creativity unhampered by our ignorance, distrust, and limitations!

Next Cognition…

Cognition 4
Utilization of the Power

"There is an invisible field of energy and information that exists beyond this three-dimensional realm of space and time—and that we have access to it."

—Dr. Joe Dispenza

"Mind in itself is believed to be a subtle form of static energy, from which arises the activities called 'thought,' which is the dynamic phase of mind. Mind is static energy; thought is dynamic energy—the two phases of the same thing."

—William Walker Atikinson

"To control circumstances a knowledge of certain scientific principles of mind-action is required."

—Charles Haanel

Who is channeling the manifestation?

Who is doing the manifestation?

As important as the discovery of electricity, an energy that was invisible until discovered and utilized, is the discovery of the Quantum (unified)Field. The Quantum Field is also an invisible field of energy and information and as discussed in Cognition 1, highly likely a field of intelligence or consciousness that exists beyond space and time. (See Cognition 1 regarding the odds of this Universe creating itself!). Some refer to it as the fifth dimension, the fourth dimension being time. This universal energy and information govern all the laws of nature. And if it is omnipresent, then it must be present within every individual. Everyone must therefore be a manifestation of this Universal Energy or Consciousness, as well as of everything that exists in the Physical Universe.[10]

What if the conversations and interactions with my inner voice and resultant personal wins and manifestations are directly related to this Intelligent Quantum Field?

What if this Energy Field or Consciousness is available to all of us as a tool to manifest our desires and/or get advice and counsel? What if the *Invisible Architect* is both our Personal Life Coach and Assistant, our Counselor and Life Architect?

What if the *Invisible Architect* actually *is* the Manifester and we are the Manifestees?

What if this Intelligent Energy is the *general* and we are the *particular*? By *particular* I mean we are individual intelligent energies—baby *Invisible Architects*—who the *Invisible Architect* expresses itself through. By *general*, I mean the Architect (Absolute), which assumes innumerable forms of manifestations (particulars) in its urge to express itself, which it does through each particular. And conversely, we channel this Intelligent Energy by inviting it to do so. It's a two-way relationship!

This could be called self-determinism, as what purpose would there be if the Architect simply bypassed us and expressed itself through each of us willy-nilly without permission? There would be no need for us!

If this is so, then our lives must always be the exact reflection of this expression of the *Absolute Spirit* through each *Particular Spirit*. Then, as our perception of this Truth approaches illumination, so does the

---

[10]So, maybe when I was growing up there was something to the teaching in catechism class that man was made in the "image and likeness of God?"

perfect life within us manifest without. This, I believe, is what the expression "as within without" means, or as Bob Proctor stated:

"The space around us is not empty. It is full of a living essence, which is like a conduit that carries our mental frequencies out into the field of possibility."

Shouldn't we want to know then how to communicate with and effectively employ this Chief Architect—the *Manifester?*

Personally, I feel blessed that I stumbled upon the *Invisible Architect* at the early age of three when I heard a voice say "that's it," referring to the black and white keys (accordion) on TV. From then on, I began paying attention to this *inner voice* more and more as my life evolved. I became so interested that I began serious study and research of the spiritual mechanics involved, leading ultimately to my desire to share my discoveries through the writing of this book, which I now know to be part of *my* Divine purpose.

Why aren't we all paying attention to this inner voice and using it as a tool to design a better life, I thought? Wouldn't the world be a better place if we became more aware of this super-intelligent consciousness—this energy that seems to permeate all things—and learn how to use it effectively to create a better world?

I'll let the physicists research the science of this, but I'll share how I have been becoming more aware of, connecting to, and using this *Intelligent Consciousne*ss effectively, as evidenced by the timeline of architect-related events I described in Cognition 2.

A little analogy first…

An electrical appliance needs the invisible energy of electricity to perform its intended functions, correct? Without electricity it doesn't work; the on switch has no effect. Also, the electric appliance has zero awareness of anything! It simply performs its intended function when turned on and operated in the correct manner by the operator. The operator must connect it to the "energy" it needs to function. The operator therefore must be aware of the appliance's performance needs in order to get the intended results. These needs are connection to the correct electricity (voltage and amps), the switch being on, and any other requirements the appliance requires to function efficiently.

So, if the *Invisible Architect* is the energy field or consciousness and the *Individual* (spirit, mind, body) is the *Appliance*, then the purpose of the *Invisible Architect* is to help us design our lives! But for this to happen, we must plug in to the *Invisible Architect*'s energy and flip the switch on just like the appliance must be plugged into the electricity (power).

The fundamentals therefore are:

1: Certainty of the existence of the *Invisible Architect*, which is achieved through observation, experience, and knowledge. Observation means viewing it in action (see my personal stories in Cognition 2), personal experience means using and interacting with this intelligent energy, and knowledge means studying how to efficiently use this power that we all have access to.[11]

2: Learning the spiritual language necessary to communicate with the *Invisible Architect*, which is focused prayer—a clear, detailed request of what one desires accompanied by a 100 percent expectation that the desired outcome has already been achieved in *your* mental garden or universe—not *will* be achieved but has already been achieved in the Quantum Energy Field, despite reality saying otherwise, as it has not yet been achieved in the manifest or Physical Universe.

3: Expressing the advance gratitude that will happen in the future when your desire is achieved in the now or in present time! This is accomplished by time traveling mentally into the future and imagining the desire achieved along with all of its emotions and life changes, and then time traveling back into the present and expressing gratitude for the desire achieved, even though in "reality" it hasn't yet been manifested in your outer world. This could be called *remembering the future*, a phrase discussed in "Becoming Supernatural" by Dr. Joe Dispenza.

Example: If your *desire* was a *more loving mother/daughter relationship*, then the focused prayer would be:

---

[11]Some of us use this intelligent energy intuitively and on a hit and miss basis but by learning these fundamentals can use it more efficiently.

"My daughter and I *have* a fantastic loving relationship! I can see us together enjoying each other and freely communicating. Our lives are whole again—tears of joy for us and the entire family! I am so happy and grateful!"

For whatever reason, when this *field of intelligence or consciousness* receives a clear request accompanied by advance gratitude, it immediately understands what you desire and begins the process of orchestrating all the conditions necessary for *your desire to manifest* in the sensory universe. This includes *your* participation and activity.

In fact, the Architect apparently has no choice in the matter, which suggests to me that this is a Law—the Law of Cause and Effect or Correspondence—meaning that for an effect to have been manifested, there had to be a corresponding cause. You cannot permanently improve any unwanted life situation (effect) without improving (altering) its cause!

Example: When I was nineteen, I began the bad habit of smoking. Within seven months, I was a chain smoker. My parents were furious with me! One day while my parents were both at work, an interesting event happened. I was practicing the piano as I usually did for six hours a day when I suddenly became aware of my awful habit. I not only had two ashtrays, one on each side of the piano, both with a lit cigarette in them, but I also had a cigarette in my mouth and the smoke was rising up into my right eye and distracting my piano practice. I thought, *What the hell am I doing? This is nuts!* The *Invisible Architect* agreed and said, "If you find the cause you can easily change this unwanted habit (effect)!" I thought, *Hmmm...how interesting!* I stopped practicing and time traveled back to the incident when I started smoking and found the why—the cause that was manifesting this unwanted behavior.

The Incident (Cause): I was a junior in high school, and the prom was coming up. I had just gotten my driver's license and really wanted to ask this girl to go with me. I wanted to show off and be cool and use my parents' car, but they said no! "You just got your license; you can go to the prom next year when you are a senior." I was devastated, and I didn't understand why they were being so mean. And once my parents said no, that was that! I stormed out of the house and went to hang with some of my friends who…guess what? Smoked! I was so mad at my parents for not allowing me to use their car that I did the one thing I knew they hated: smoking cigarettes! They had no bad habits like smoking, drinking, or doing drugs. They were good people, good role models. I asked one of my friends to give me one of his Pall Mall cigarettes. I choked and choked, but I was determined to inhale and become a smoker just to get back at my parents for not allowing me to use their car for the junior prom.

A year and a half later while practicing the piano, I became aware of the reason why I had started my nasty smoking habit by following the Architect's advice and traveling back to the past incident (cause) as mentioned above; I then traveled back to the present, laughed, got up from the piano, put out the burning cigarettes that were distracting my piano practice, grabbed the remaining carton, and threw it in the garbage. There were no nicotine withdrawals, nothing. It was easy, and I never smoked again!

In hindsight, I redirected my energy (attention) to the root cause—the decision to get back at my parents by smoking—not the actual cigarette smoking (unwanted effect in the outer world), and it was easy and natural to quit smoking immediately! Why? Because my smoking was a lie in the first place! I personally had no interest in smoking—it was a revenge decision, a protest that once uncovered made it easy for me to affirm *don't smoke* and change the cause, which was manifesting the bad habit in my outer world. It was an instantaneous manifestation![12] As within, without!

----

[12]Note: Although finding the cause made the process easier, I really didn't need to time travel back to the cause-event, which sometimes can be very difficult without a guide. I could have just repetitively affirmed "I don't smoke; I have no interest in smoking" and then imagined not smoking and all of the feelings associated with not smoking, my parents thanking me for quitting, my better health, etc. and gave advance gratitude that I no longer smoked. This is the Be-Do-Have Sequence, which we will discuss in more detail in the following Cognition. (Sandi Anders, *The "Be Do Have" Paradigm: Attracting What You Want.*)

Q&A Cognition 4

1. Q: Do I have access to this invisible field of energy and information that exists beyond space and time?
   A: Yes, you do, but your efficacy employing it is contingent on your understanding and application of certain scientific principles.[13]

2. Q: How does the Architect work with you?
   A: The Architect is the general; you are the particular! Its urge is to know itself by self-expression through you, and conversely you channel this awesome intelligent energy by inviting it to do so through your desires. It's a two-way relationship.

3. Q: How do you achieve certainty that the *Invisible Architect* is real?
   A: Through observation, experience, and knowledge.

4. Q: What is focused prayer?
   A: A clear, detailed request to the *Invisible Architect*, accompanied by the 100 percent expectation that your desired request has already been achieved despite reality saying otherwise.

5. Q: What is advance gratitude?
   A: Gratitude that will naturally happen in the future when your desire is fulfilled but expressed in advance in the present!

---

[13] I am positive we are all on a spiritual journey to return to a state of unity with the Divine—the Invisible Architect. But to achieve this unity or illumination, we must each aspire to do so. This is known as spiritual growth.

6. Q: How is advance gratitude done?
   A: It is done by time traveling mentally into the future and imagining the desire achieved along with all of its emotions and changes in your life, and then time traveling back into the present and expressing gratitude for the wish fulfilled, even though in "reality" it hasn't yet been manifested in your outer world. This could be called *remembering the future*.

7. Q: How can you change and improve any unwanted circumstance in your outer world?
   A: You must change its cause, which always exists in your inner world. For any effect—good or bad—to have manifested in the Physical Universe, there is always a corresponding cause in your personal mental universe. (See Cognition 6: The Different Universes.)

Can you think of any unwanted outer world situations that you would love to improve? If so, write them down and have at them one at a time! It's fun and productive once you get the hang of it; you are designing your life from within—congrats!

Next Cognition…

Cognition 5
Be-Do-Have Sequence

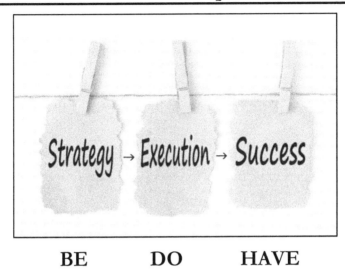

BE   DO   HAVE

"You have to BE before you can DO and DO before you can HAVE"

—*Zig Ziglar*

"Nobody cares how much you know, until they know how much you care."

—*Theodore Roosevelt*

"There is a Divine Design for each person, something that you are to do which no one else can do. There is a perfect picture of this in your higher self or God mind and usually flashes across your consciousness as an unobtainable ideal—something too good to be true."

—*Florence Scovel Shinn*

One of my most useful cognitions was my discovery and understanding of the Be-Do Have-Sequence and how to apply it to the achievement of my desires. In my opinion, to be, to do, and to have are three Divine gifts from the *Invisible Architect*. This mindset sequence is the fundamental principle of manifestation—Law of Attraction, and not understanding this sequence is the main reason people struggle achieving their desires.

BE is desire—your strategy. Desire, according to Joseph Murphy, the pioneer of success thinking, is behind all progress.

It is the push of the Life-Principle. It is an angel of God telling us something that, if accepted by us, will make our life fuller and happier. DO is the execution—everything that needs to be accomplished to achieve success—the HAVE!

$$BE + DO = HAVE$$

$$STRATEGY + EXECUTION = SUCCESS$$

Personally, I think we are all perfect beings implanted with positive desires, urges to survive in abundance, and to help others do the same. But through ignorance, a person may misdirect his desires. For example, a desire to be wealthy with no personal growth—a desire that would have to be made by someone with their head not screwed on straight—could after many failed attempts (frustration) be misdirected to such an extent that this person becomes a thief, goes down the dark side, and eventually self-destructs! I don't think this is Satan or some demon inhabiting us to do evil, as is often stated; it is simply our decision to do so through ignorance. It is a perversion of the power! We have free will and self-determinism, as it should be.

In the *Master Key System,* Haanel says:

"If you use electricity for light, you call it good. If you grasp a wire which has not been properly insulated and it kills you, it is not for that reason bad or evil. You were simply careless or ignorant of the laws governing electricity. For the same reason, the one Infinite Power, which is the source of all Power, manifests in your life either as good or as evil, as you make use of it constructively or destructively."

It is irresponsible to assign causation to any person, entity, or outside source.

In other words, *we* choose to go down the dark side. And I know, some may disagree; but what would be the logic of creating a paradigm with an all-knowing, all-loving, all-powerful *Intelligent Energy Field* and then pitting that force against its antithesis? That would violate freedom of choice and self-determinism and hardly be an ethical game worth participating in. But educate a person on spiritual mechanics—that we all have an *Invisible Architect* that can help us achieve our desires—then anyone can overcome any frustration and/or opposition and succeed! Yes, it takes responsibility and work ethic, but that is a good thing and the way out of our self-imposed jail.

The purpose of this book is to simply share cognitions I have had on my personal life's journey with the hope that they may help you on yours—not to prove the existence of monotheism or pantheism.

So how can *you* use this gift of Be-Do-Have to design your life? First, you must really understand an emotion called *love*. What is this thing called love? (Great jazz standard by the way!)

There have been many poems, writings, and quotes about the power of love. I suggest you look them up, as they are very inspirational. I have, as we all do, my own wonderful experiences with love.

One of my favorites is:

"Only love knows love and love knows only love." —Neville Goddard

It is said that God is Love; Love is God. What I understand that to mean is God—*the Invisible Architect*—imparts its *Beingness of Divinity* through human expression. This self-giving to us is the ultimate expression of love—to give of oneself!

As a sidebar, one of the greatest composers ever, Johann Sebastian Bach, said that music was for the glorification of God. Given his prolific output and the Divine nature of his music, I'd say he was totally in touch with the *Invisible Architect*, allowing it to express itself perfectly through his amazing work ethic and talent.

There is one mind, the Universal Mind, which is Spirit. You are Spirit, I am Spirit, Spirit is Spirit—we are all Spirit. The *Invisible Architect* is therefore in everyone; the two points of view are one! The interaction between these two viewpoints—*God-Creation* and *Individual-Creation*—is the spiritual mechanics of the Law of Attraction!

Now how this knowledge and the Be-Do-Have sequence is utilized in designing our lives from within is quite interesting and downright miraculous!

Let's say you have a goal of being financially affluent. That's the HAVE... The next step is determining what you would have to BE-come (BE), which when accomplished will trigger or dictate your imagination and supporting actions—the DOs—and cause the *Invisible Architect* to work its magic! The correct sequence therefore would be to become one with the BE. Becoming one with a person or thing is *love*! There would be no distance or separation between the *lover* and the "*lovee*"! As an example, in a loving relationship, the feeling of love and oneness is wonderful, but if a problem enters the relationship, that wonderful feeling becomes lost, and there's a perception of distance or separation, of incompleteness and *not-being*. In other words, something is broken until the problem, the separation, is resolved and the affinity restored!

Or how about being one with a musical instrument like the piano? Your love is so great that when you play, you are the piano, and the piano is you! Athletes call that *being in the zone*!

There are an infinite number of examples. Can you think of any?

So, if the goal is to achieve financial affluence, you would have to *be one with financial affluence*, first in your inner world and then in your outer world. You would operate as a financially affluent person would—no stress about finances, see abundance everywhere, imagining your life as a financially affluent person, seeing yourself in your new house, your car, new clothes, what your friends would be saying about you, etc. You would attune yourself to that financially affluent *frequency* and not to your current lower *frequency* of financial limitation and scarcity. You would plant the financially affluent seed in your mental garden (universe) and expect its fruition in the garden of reality (the Physical Universe), and most importantly, you would ignore anybody or anything, even your own senses, that tell you otherwise. You cannot create a new reality if you simply stay in contact with and validate the undesired reality—the reality you want to change. It doesn't work that way. You will just get more of the same, and if you think about it for a while, I think you will agree.

You must become (BE) ONE with the desired reality—financial affluence—until your faith and consciousness of the new reality is 100 percent believed. This is pure love! Then and only then does the *Invisible Architect* go to work attracting the necessary relationships and situations in your life that lead you into the decisions and actions (DO) that will create the new desired reality (Have)—financial affluence!

So to review, BE is *love of* or *oneness with* the goal; DO is the imagination of the goal achieved in all its glory along with *action toward* the goal assisted by *the Invisible Architect's* rearranging of the Quantum Energy Field to attract what is needed; and HAVE is the goal or *desire fulfilled*, amen![14] Now why and how the *Invisible Architect* assists us in designing our lives is a miracle unto itself, but from my experience, it simply uses all the natural laws, channels, existing energy, communication lines, thoughts, and other people in the Physical Universe to orchestrate and manifest our desires. Quite brilliant and yet another proof of the Supernatural at work!

The key, though, and the main part of DO, is that the goal achieved has to be assumed as already completed in *your* mental garden—your mental universe—with all the appropriate *feeling* and *gratitude* that would (will) happen in the garden of reality—the manifest or Physical Universe!

You must understand that the Physical Universe is totally different than your personal universe. Otherwise, when your desire doesn't instantly manifest in your outer world, you will incorrectly conclude that things aren't working which is false! This will lead to frustrations and all manner of upsets, leading you potentially to give up and/or possibly go to the dark side.

---

[14] This is the mechanics of the Law of Attraction; not understanding these spiritual mechanics is why many fail! (Dr Joseph Murphy, *To Be, To Do & To Have.*)

My next personal cognition, therefore, was understanding spiritual mechanics and their interaction with the different universes, which for me was the missing manifestation fundamental.

Q&A Cognition 5

1. Q: What does "Whatsoever ye shall ask in my name, that I will do" mean?
   A: It means whatever your desire is (to Be), clearly ask the *Invisible Architect* for it, and if you understand the spiritual mechanics, it shall be delivered.

2. Q: What are the three Divine gifts?
   A: To Be, to Do, to Have are three Divine gifts from the *Invisible Architect* given to us to help us design our lifestyle. They are analogous to Strategy, Execution, and Success!

3. Q: Why can it be reasoned that there is probably one Infinite Intelligence or Ordering Power?
   A: Please explain in your own words...

4. Q: What is meant by God is Love; Love is God?
   A: God, the *Invisible Architect*, imparts its Beingness of Divinity through human expression. This *self-giving* to us is the ultimate expression of affinity (love)—to give of oneself! And what a wonderful world this would be if we did the same!

5. Q: What is the definition of Be, Do, and Have?
   A: Be is love of or oneness with; Do is action toward the goal assisted by the *Invisible Architect*'s rearranging of the quantum energy field; and Have is the goal or wish fulfilled.

6. Think of as many examples as you can of being ONE with—total affinity with—a person, desire, skill, situation, thing, etc.

Next Cognition...

Cognition 6
The Different Universes

"I am the Person that Thou art," and "Thou art the Person that I am."

—*Thomas Troward "The Hidden Power"*

This cognition, as with all cognitions, is mostly empirical in nature, as science hasn't yet fully comprehended and correlated the mathematics of Quantum physics as it relates to spiritual mechanics—the relationship between the Universal Consciousness and its creations and the interactions thereof.

Personally, though, I have observed and experienced the following paradigm to be quite consistent:

The *Invisible Architect* manifested all there is by *creative thought*! How and why is speculation, but I imagine that as I become more *illumined*, which as mentioned earlier I believe is the purpose of life on this plane, the answer will become more and more self-evident.

This *Invisible Architect* is not a separate being existing in some other dimension and commanding us to be good and worship it, but more of an *Intelligent Energy field* that is not only the Prime Cause of everything but also permeates everything—matter, energy, space, and time, including all life. That also means you and me! This *Intelligent Energy* is therefore probably a composite consciousness made up collectively of all life. We are harmonics of the *Invisible Architect*. The Architect is made complete by expressing itself through its creations, and we are made more complete as we become more and more aware of this Divine relationship and in turn express ourselves through *our* creations.

We could call this being illumined or enlightened. Our desires are fulfilled by allowing and channeling this *perfect omniscient energy* through us to design our lives!

The *Invisible Architect* is us; we are the *Invisible Architect*!

We are one; we are Spirit!

Pretty blasphemous, I know, but at the same time a miraculous cognition that when understood and applied produces spectacular results!

Ask and you shall receive; don't ask and you shall not receive.

Apparently, we have self-determinism in this game called life. How refreshing and thoughtful. The *Invisible Architect* can only work its magic if you are clear in your prayer. Ask for its fulfillment and honestly believe and have advance gratitude in the now that the wish is fulfilled, and so shall it be. This is the language of manifestation![15]

---

[15]"And all things, whatsoever ye shall ask in prayer, believing, ye shall receive."
—Matthew 21:22

Be + Do = Have.

A word to the wise: Be careful what you clearly ask for or affirm, as it will begin manifesting instantly proportional to your belief so…deny the bad, see only the good!

The following affirmation repeated nightly before falling asleep will raise your frequency and enhance all desires to manifest:

"Invisible Architect, cause me to only see perfection in everything I am, I do, and I have!"

It seems that the *Invisible Architect* seeks to know itself—to attain absolute knowledge of itself—by willingly expressing itself through us, thereby helping us manifest our desires. I know as a composer that rings true, as the more I compose and perform, the more I understand who I am. By inviting the Architect into our personal universes, we acquaint ourselves with perfection and not only achieve our desires, but accordingly achieve enlightenment on the way!

The ultimate achievement then would be ONENESS with the *Invisible Architect* by knowingly and causatively alternating our beingness with it— an amazing goal, don't you think? We do this through the gift of thinking: thought. Thought is the purest and clearest energy—light energy. Our minds create thought and are electromagnetic systems that exist outside of space and time. The universe could be said to be a vast collection of thoughts provided by minds that can think both individually and collectively.

Each mind is itself a *Particular* Individual Architect, and the collection of all minds is the *Absolute Invisible Architect*!

Important Definitions:

Universe: 1. All created things viewed as constituting one system or whole; the world; e.g., the Physical Universe; 2. Any whole body or collection of things, or of phenomena; e.g., a person's universe; a particular sphere of activity, interest, or experience; e.g., the universe of mathematics, atoms, music, insects, oceans, spiritual universe, etc.

There are many Universes, but the following are important for understanding the spiritual mechanics of designing our lives.

1. The *Invisible Architect* Universe
2. Thought Universe
3. Personal Universe
4. Manifest Universe

Invisible Architect Universe: An intelligent energy field that is not only the Cause or Supreme Source of everything but also permeates everything. It is perfect light, perfect reason, perfect knowledge, perfect understanding, perfect symmetry, perfect consciousness, and perfect bliss. If you go into the Silence and close your eyes and imagine you are omniscient—the highest type of perception—and you do this daily especially before you fall asleep, when the conscious mind is at its lowest activity, you will be raising your frequency to the God-Frequency. Only then will you "acquaint" yourself with the Universe from which everything comes. Enlightenment—even if temporary—could be defined as matching this God-Frequency and being at peace.

Thought Universe: If the *Invisible Architect* is an "intelligent energy" whose Omniscient Creative Thought brought the Physical Universe into being and we are harmonics of the *Invisible Architect*, then we too have this exact creative ability but on a lesser scale. Our thoughts are directed energy; they are our *minds in motion*; they are creative, and so they can create realities in the thought universe that can be manifested in the Physical Universe. For anything to be created in the Physical Universe, it must be created in one's thought universe first—there must be an archetype in the thought universe, i.e., a building is first designed to exact specs for a clear reason—that is, its blueprint, which can then be used to create the building in the Physical Universe. It starts, however, with the thought of a building. Any thought, therefore, under certain conditions can create a reality!

Personal Universe: Each of us, from human to amoeba, has its own unique universe created from our personal thoughts and channelings of the *Invisible Architect.*

Manifest or Physical Universe: The Physical Universe is the Architect's Creative Thought. It brought the Physical Universe into manifestation just as our worlds (universes) are created by our thoughts. You either believe this or not, or maybe you're not sure. Or maybe you believe it was an accident or a big bang. For me, based on my personal experiences as discussed earlier and observing the Physical Universe and all of its grandeur, abundance, infinity, and interconnecting laws and the miracle of life itself and all of its infinite permutations, well...that's proof enough for me to believe in or postulate the existence of an Intelligent Consciousness, a Quantum Field, or whatever we have named it over time that created the Physical Universe. The more important considerations are...

- How does one feel when you have personal faith in the existence of the Architect?
- Can you use this faith to connect to the Architect?
- Can employing the Architect improve your life and the life of others?

Personally, I cannot imagine disconnecting from the knowledge and power of the *Invisible Architect* for one second! It would be like a soldier in battle disconnecting from his platoon and command center and trying to defeat the enemy by himself and with no weapons or ammo! Now, if you were a soldier who had amnesia and didn't know you were part of an army with a purpose, well, then, you'd be in the same trouble as the soldier with no backup or weapons, and therein lies the situation with many of us. We are ignorant of our spiritual nature and connection with the *Invisible Architect* and thus go through life haphazardly by ourselves, which is not ideal![16]

---

[16]"I am the Person that Thou art," and "Thou art the Person that I am. Continual Alternating between these two Viewpoints is THE Basic Truth. The

Q&A Cognition 6

1. Q: What does Troward mean when he states: "I am the Person that Thou art," and "Thou art the Person that I am. Continual Alternating between these two Viewpoints is THE Basic Truth."?

   A: This *Invisible Architect* is not a separate being existing in some dimension. The *Invisible Architect* is us; we are the *Invisible Architect!* We are One!

2. Q: Define the *Invisible Architect.*

   A: The Universal Consciousness that created all there is by creative thought. As we become more enlightened, which I believe is the purpose of life in this dimension, the answer to why this is so will become self-evident.

3. Q: Why is it important to be careful what you ask for or affirm?

   A: Because whatever your dominant thought is, it will begin manifesting immediately even if not readily perceived.

4. Q: How do you achieve oneness with the *Invisible Architect?*

   A: By knowingly and causatively through thought—the purest and clearest light energy—alternating *your* beingness with the *Invisible Architect*'s Beingness.

5. Q: If each mind is an Individual Architect, what is the collection of all minds?

   A: The Absolute *Invisible Architect!*

6. Q: There are many universes, but which ones are most important to understand in order to understand and apply the spiritual mechanics of designing your life from within?

Two Personalities are One" —Thomas Troward, "The Hidden Power"

A: The God Universe, the thought universe, your personal universe, and the manifest or Physical Universe.

7. Define each one of these universes in your own words.

8. Q: Why do most people go through life haphazardly?
   A: They are not only ignorant of their spiritual essence and thus connection to the *Invisible Architect*, but they also lack the know-how—spiritual development—to employ the *Invisible Architect* in the designing of their lives (spiritual mechanics).

Next Cognition…

Cognition 7
Everything Is Energy
(The Law of Attraction)

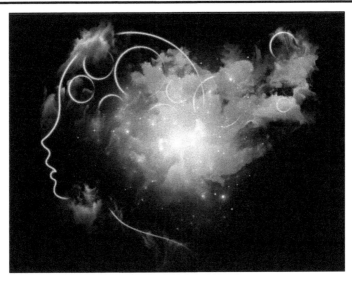

"The cosmos is within us. We are made of star-stuff. We are a way for the universe to know itself."

—Carl Sagan

"In our quest for happiness and the avoidance of suffering, we are all fundamentally the same, and therefore equal. Despite the characteristics that differentiate us—race, language, religion, gender, wealth and many others—we are all equal in terms of our basic humanity."

—Dalai Lama

"Every particular in nature, a leaf, a drop, a crystal, a moment of time is related to the whole, and partakes of the perfection of the whole." —Ralph Waldo Emerson

—Ralph Waldo Emerson

**Everything Is Energy Your
Thoughts Begin the Process
Your Emotions Amplify the Process
Your Supportive Actions Increase Momentum**

You have probably heard of the Law of Attraction, which was made popular by the movie *The Secret*. It is based on the idea that everything—matter, space, people, and their thoughts—are all made from pure energy. Through the process of attraction, whereby like energy attracts like energy, and frequency matching, we can attract our desires. In other words, you electromagnetically attract things that are vibrating on the same frequency as you are. This means that if you work to maintain a high frequency (through positivity, love, compassion, health, wealth, or productivity), then you inevitably attract more of these good things into your life.[17]

Make sense?

In the 1900s, beliefs about physical reality changed with the beginnings of quantum physics. This new science proves that the universe, including us, is made up of energy, not matter. Everything is composed of energy.

The energy that makes you is the same energy that composes trees, rocks, the chair you are sitting on, your phone, and your computer or tablet which you are using to read this book. It's all made of the same stuff: energy. Therefore, it is not a big leap to assume that since we are all composed of the same energy, we are all connected. We are therefore all *one*, which sets the stage for the Law of Attraction—also known as the Law of Cause and Effect.

The Law of Attraction works with energy to help manifest our desires. This has some incredible implications; it has led to *quantum spirituality*, a set of metaphysical beliefs and associated practices that seek to relate

---

[17] "An assumption—whether conscious or unconscious—builds a bridge of incidents that lead inevitably to the fulfillment of itself." —Neville Goddard, *The Power of Imagination*.

consciousness, intelligence, spirituality, or mystical worldviews to the ideas of quantum mechanics and its interpretations.[18]

The great American theoretical physicist, John Archibald Wheeler, postulated that we live in a "participatory universe," which emerges from the interplay of consciousness and physical reality, the subjective and objective realms. Wheeler suggested that reality is created by observers and that "no phenomenon is a real phenomenon until it is an observed phenomenon." He coined the term "participatory anthropic principle" (PAP) from the Greek *anthropos* for "human." He went on further to suggest that "we are participants in bringing into being not only the near and here, but the far away and long ago." As you can see from some of my experiences (stated in Cognition 2), I couldn't agree more. I not only envisioned, almost every day, my song "Good to Go" going to number one on the Billboard jazz chart, I even took a real Billboard jazz chart and pasted my song at the top and *observed* it as much as possible. So, I guess you could say that is an example of using the participatory anthropic principle! (Suggest review stories in Cognition 2)

---

[18]"In quantum physics, objects are possibilities residing in a domain of potentiality outside of space and time. In this domain, no signals are required for communication when two objects are in a state of correlation or entanglement; communication is instantaneous. Such instant communication is forbidden in space and time, where communication must take place through an exchange of signals, and that has a speed limit. Communication takes a little time for signals to go through the distance that separates the objects. In contrast, the domain of non-locality — signal-less communication — is a domain of potential unity. Closer examination reveals that this domain of potential unity is consciousness and its potentialities. And the domain of space and time is what consciousness experiences by becoming immanent and separating itself into a self (subject) and the other (objects) in the process of converting potentiality into manifestation." Quantum Spirituality by Amit Goswami, PhD | Jun 21, 2019 | https://www.amitgoswami.org/2019/06/21/quantum-spirituality/

American author and philosopher Charles Haanel, who is best known for his contributions to the New Thought movement, states the following in his renowned series of lessons (1912), *The Master Key System*, which I highly recommend studying:

"There is a world within—a world of thought and feeling and power; of light and life and beauty and, although invisible, its forces are mighty."

"The world within is governed by mind. When we discover this world, we shall find the solution for every problem, the cause for every effect; and since the world within is subject to our control, all laws of power and possession are also within our control."

"The world without reflects the world within. What appears without is what has been found within. In the world within may be found infinite Wisdom, infinite Power, infinite Supply of all that is necessary, waiting for unfoldment, development, and expression. If we recognize these potentialities in the world within, they will take form in the world without."

"The world without reflects the circumstances and conditions of our consciousness within."

Quantum physics proves that solid matter does not exist in the universe on the quantum level. Although solid objects are perceptible to the senses, their constituents are actually from energy at the quantum level, which is not perceptible to our senses. In basic physics, it is clear that atoms are not solid; in fact, they have three main subatomic particles inside of them: protons, neutrons, and electrons.[19] The protons and

---

[19] There are thirty-six confirmed fundamental particles, including anti-particles, according to Professor Craig Savage, from the Australian National University. Twelve of these are the force-carrying particles: the photon, the weak force carriers W-, W+, Z0, and the eight gluons. This set also includes the anti-particles. The other twenty-four are called matter particles and only interact with each other indirectly via the force carriers. These include three types of

neutrons are packed together into the center of the atom, while the electrons whiz around the outside. The electrons move so quickly that we never know exactly where they are from one moment to the next. The atoms that form objects and substances, which we call solid, are actually made up of 99.99999 percent space.

Einstein's theories make abundantly clear that the universe is composed of energy. Einstein posited that $E=mc^2$. The implications of this formulation are enormous and profound. The equation $E=mc^2$ explains that, under the right conditions, matter becomes energy and energy becomes matter. So, what we perceive as solid matter is mostly empty space with a pattern of energy permeating it. This principle can be extended to the expectations of the observer, too. According to Heisenberg's *Uncertainty Principle*, as experiments have confirmed, the elementary particles, in this energy, are affected by observation.

So, given that science has proven that there are particles of energy all around us that coalesce to create matter, our mental events are also composed of energy, including our thoughts, intentions, words, and actions. We create manifestations through thoughts, words, and actions. These use energy to form objects, conditions, and experiences. Quantum physics has discovered that not only do particles consist of energy, but so does the space between them. They refer to this as zero-point energy.

Therefore, everything consists of energy. And what if energy isn't just random energy? What if there is an *Intelligent All-Ordering Energy?*

If everything therefore is energy, then everything is connected and not separate. If this is so, then we *are* essentially ONE even though we are unique beings with different energy signatures. In other words, our

---

neutrino, three types of electron-like particles, six types of quark, and the twelve associated anti-particles.

energy (thought), especially when focused, affects other energy systems in some manner.[20]

One could therefore hypothesize that in the beginning, there must have been a *Creator* or *Intelligent Energy* that, for whatever reason—Boy, would I like to know that reason—directed a thought or sequence of thoughts, which manifested into the Physical Universe. Similarly, we direct our thoughts to create the realities that we desire. In doing so, we have yet another example of the God-nature within us.

We could say then that creation is an inside job! The *Invisible Architect* is in each of us and available to us to help design our lives. Our inner world creates our outer world; our thoughts create our realities.

As a simple experiment before going to bed, close your eyes and put your attention on something; for example, something you desire to improve. Let's say you have a scarcity of time and money. Okay, now put your attention on the higher frequencies of success, including affluence and an abundance of financial freedom, as well as time freedom. Concentrate on these higher frequencies, instead of the lower frequencies of failure, struggle, and scarcity—and of having not enough. At first it may be difficult to concentrate on these positive concepts, especially if your life has been filled with a scarcity of the things that you desire, or if you are struggling and extremely stressed. Continue to do this exercise every night, and soon your imagination will begin to attract more and more high-energy ideas, and you will begin falling asleep at higher frequencies. You will not only get a better night's sleep, but you will wake up physically and mentally refreshed. You will be at a higher frequency to attack and create your day instead of being passive while the day creates you!

This simple assignment can be extended as follows. Whenever you become aware that your attention is stuck in toxic lower frequencies and

---

[20]The Beatles may have been onto something with their lyrics: "I am he as you are he as you are me and we are all together." — "I Am the Walrus," by Lennon & McCartney

negative emotions, immediately substitute their opposite higher frequency counterparts. For example, say you're worrying about your mortgage or rent. Suppose that you are behind in payments. The moment you become aware of your stuck energy on that subject, substitute in its place the opposite thought, which would be something like this: "My mortgage is totally caught up, as I have plenty of money to pay it and all of my bills!"

Now, you may get some pushback from your objective mind, telling you that it isn't so! Ignore that pushback! Obliterate it! The physical collective reality is rearing its ugly head. You must simply differentiate universes. The Physical Universe is separate from your personal thought universe. And since *your* thoughts and beliefs have something to do with creating your realities in the Physical Universe, you can change the unwanted condition in your outer world by changing your thoughts. As a starting point, change your thoughts and beliefs from within your personal universe. This exercise does exactly that.

In the Physical Universe, there's a law that no two objects can occupy the same space at the same time.[21] There is a law in the thought universe, too, according to which no two thoughts can occupy the same space at the same time. By mastering your personal thoughts and beliefs, which takes a little practice and discipline, and keeping them predominantly positive (or higher frequency in nature), you will be able to replace thoughts of a lower vibration. You will not only feel better most of the time, given the positive effect of higher frequency thoughts, but you will also tend electromagnetically to attract positive emotions, ideas, solutions, and better life situations.

---

[21]Exception: Particles have spins. Particles that have integer spin are called *bosons* and *can* occupy the same space at the same time, meaning the probability of finding one in an (x,y,z) coordinate increases the more of them there are. Bosons can occupy the same quantum state in general. Particles with half integer spin are *fermions* and follow the fermi-dirac statistics, and thus cannot occupy the same space; i.e., the probability of finding one in an (x,y,z) spot will always be the probability for finding one particle; only one can occupy a quantum state at a time, in general. Anna Serphimidou Vayaki (Anna V). Retired experimental particle physicist.

This process works. You can prove it to yourself by doing the suggested exercises frequently.

Here is a real-life example of how frequency creates attraction or repulsion. Do you like being around someone who is constantly complaining and being critical of everything? Do you feel good around these kinds of toxic people? They usually bring you down, as these lower emotional frequencies tend to attract more of the same, and thus they lower your own frequency if you allow that to happen. By contrast, to be around incredibly positive people can be inspirational, as their higher frequencies tend to attract more of the same, and thus they raise your own emotional frequency, too!

Our thoughts, therefore, are catalysts for self-perpetuating cycles. They can directly influence how we feel, which influences our decisions, actions, behavior and believe it or not, our bodily harmony and functions! If you think you're depressed, you'll begin feeling depressed, relative to your predominant thoughts. If you think you are successful and act as if you are, you'll begin feeling happy![22]

Have you ever been around people who seem to live a cursed life where anything that can go wrong does? Their normal routine includes being late, missing flights, and getting fired. They suffer from flat tires, equipment not working, frequent sickness, bounced checks, broken relationships, and other misfortunes. These negative experiences seem to be the norm! Do you think their thoughts and beliefs might have something do with their bad luck? I do, because when a person like this changes their mindset, their life begins to improve. By "mindset," I mean the collection of thoughts and beliefs that shape the way one operates.

Thoughts turn into beliefs, and beliefs turn into actions, which can be positive or negative. So, by improving the quality and focus of your thoughts, better decisions and actions follow as a natural

---

[22] Integrative psychiatrist James Lake, MD, of Stanford University, writes that "extensive research has confirmed the medical and mental benefits of meditation, mindfulness training, yoga, and other mind-body practices."

consequence and contribute to fulfilling your desires and thus help design your life from within.

The three steps, just described, can be summarized as: Be, Do, and Have.

It's the Be-Do-Have Sequence!
Everything Is Energy!

We live in a fathomless sea of energy mind substance. This energy is sensitive to the highest degree. It takes form *according* to our mental demand. Thought forms the matrix from which the substance expresses itself. Our ideal vision is the mold from which our future will emerge. All things are the result, in some way, of our inner process of thought and intention.

By concentration, we make the *connection* between the finite and the Infinite, the limited and the unlimited, the visible and the invisible, the personal and the impersonal. Throughout the entire universe, the Law of Cause and Effect is ever at work.

This law is supreme; here a cause, there an effect. They can never operate independently. They are twins.

Therefore, to change any unwanted effect (a condition in the outer world), one must change its cause (a condition in the inner world)! This law describes the *Invisible Architect* at work.

Question: To Be or Not to Be?

Answer: Be Whatever You *Will* to Be!

Q&A Cognition 7

1. Q: Why is it important to cultivate high-frequency states composed of positivity, success, abundance, love, compassion, health, and productivity?
   A: Because like frequencies attract like frequencies. You will feel better and better. Most important, you are frequency-matching with the *Invisible Architect*, and thereby becoming one with the ONE. That is a good thing when it comes to designing your life!

2. Q: What are the ramifications of that fact that everything is energy?
   A: Through the Law of Attraction, we can make use of this energy to help manifest our desires.

3. Q: What is Quantum Spirituality?
   A: A set of metaphysical beliefs and associated practices that seek to relate consciousness, intelligence, spirituality, or mystical worldviews to the ideas of quantum mechanics and its interpretations.

4. Q: If everything therefore is energy, what does it mean then that everything is connected and not separate?
   A: It means that we *are* essentially ONE even though we are unique beings with different energy signatures. In other words, our thoughts, a form of energy, affect other energy systems in some manner.

5. Q: What value is there in knowing that no two thoughts can occupy the same space at the same time?
   A: It means that if you find your mind fixed on any lower frequency or negative thoughts, you can simply substitute a different, more positive thought in its place.

6. Q: Why is being around people who are constantly expressing negative emotions toxic to your life?
    A: Because lower frequency emotions attract more of the same, and if you let them, they will bring your frequency down. A lower frequency separates you from the *Invisible Architect* and stops you from carrying out your desires.

7. Q: Are all things the result in some way of the thought process?
    A: Yes, your thoughts, if clear and focused, employ the *Invisible Architect* efficiently to reorganize the Quantum Field toward your desires.

8. Q: What is the best way to change any unwanted circumstance in your life?
    A: Change its cause, the condition in your inner world, to the desired cause!

9. Q: In terms of this book's theme, what is the answer to the question: "To be or not to be"?
    A: Be whatever you will to be.

10. Can you think of any creation or manifestation that didn't come from a thought, desire or belief?

Next Cognition…

Cognition 8
The Fundamentals of Manifestation (Be-Do-Have Sequence Continued)

"Disciplined or controlled imagination is one of the primal faculties of mind and has the power to project and clothe your ideas, giving them visibility of the screen of space."

—*Joseph Murphy*

"By believing passionately in something that still does not exist, we create it. The nonexistent is whatever we have not sufficiently desired."

—*Franz Kafka*

If the *Invisible Architect* (the Intelligent Energy Field) created everything there is, then we are part of that creation. It follows, therefore, that the *Invisible Architect* most likely exists within us and as a part of us and everything there is. Now, does that mean we may have that same creative power? I believe the answer is yes!

1. Thoughts rule emotions, which govern decisions, which motivate actions and create our realities.
2. Like thoughts (including emotions, beliefs, intentions) attract the same.

3. Movie screen analogy: If you, the operator of a projector, are projecting a film onto the screen, then to change the movie, it would be your job to change the reel. Now, if you did not like the movie, you wouldn't walk up to the screen and shake your hand at it, criticize it, or attack it. The screen is the wrong target. No, you would go to the source of the picture because *you* are the operator of the projector. Simply change the reel content to the movie you desire. To use another analogy, you are the scriptwriter. So, if you don't like your life's story, write a new one! That is not only your right, but it's also within your ability.

But first, you must become conscious (or aware) that you, indeed, are writing *your* story, right? Translation: If your reality is non-optimal, you can change it and write a better life script!

How?

My experience with the manifestation process is as follows:

Mindset (BE) + Mechanics (DO) = Desire Fulfilled (HAVE)

Process:

1. BE (DESIRE): Write down your desire as a completed statement. (Note: This is a different mindset from the ordinary, in which you may tend to think that your desire is impossible to achieve, or you may be hoping it can be achieved in the future.)
2. DO (IMAGINATION): Visualize and imagine your desire as already achieved and act accordingly—as if it has been done!
3. HAVE (GRATITUDE): Give thanks *now in the present* that your desire is achieved.

Desire:

Any desire, small or large, should be taken seriously. I believe that the *Invisible Architect* seeks to learn more about itself, through self-expression, through each of us. So, don't ignore desires that are positive and constructive! But those desires that are not productive can be discarded. For example, if your desire to be wealthy leads you to become a thief, that desire is misleading. (Well, that's another book's topic because the destructive thoughts that led you to steal are not coming from your inner voice; they are most likely perversions through ignorance.)

Once your desire is written down in detail as a goal, convert it into a statement of fact that is already accomplished, even though in the garden of reality, the Physical Universe, your perceptions say otherwise. Note: State your desire in the positive, not the negative. For example, instead of intending "to be debt free in one year," state your desire in the positive as follows:

Goal: "To earn enough income to handle all my demands."

Goal Redefined (as an already achieved desire): "I now earn enough money to handle all my responsibilities." Or if you want to be more accurate (which is always better): "I now consistently earn a lavish income from all my sources of income, which is more than enough to handle all my responsibilities!"

Or:

Goal: "I wish my rheumatoid arthritis to be healed!"

Goal Redefined: "My rheumatoid arthritis is healed. I am healthy!"

You get the idea?

Imagination:

Use of your imagination is *being* the Architect. You assume the point of view of the Architect, as discussed earlier. Why? Because its point of view is always perfection. By connecting your personal *thought* universe to the Architect's *thought* universe, everything and anything become possible! You can now create any desire you want, pretty much instantly! And that's the whole secret to the so-called *secret* because, as we established earlier, everything is energy. Spiritual substance (i.e., energy) is all around us, waiting to be formed and observed into reality. So, the mental picture of fulfillment, which you create *instantly* with your imagination, will compel the picture into being by attracting similar frequencies in the quantum energy field: the right situations, people, ideas, events, or coincidences will be drawn to you by your imagination. All desires, in other words, *already* exist as "unorganized potential energies and frequencies"—elementary particles, as scientists call them—awaiting direction and organization from the thought energy universe (i.e., the subjective universe) to manifest in the Physical Universe (i.e., the objective universe). This is what is meant in saying that one's inner world creates one's outer world or that your thoughts create reality.

Mastering this process gives you more control over circumstances or conditions, proportionate to the clarity of your thoughts and the application of the process.

Gratitude:

Now Gratitude: Giving thanks for everything already in your life every day creates a happy mindset. By contrast, dwelling on everything unwanted or unachieved in your life is a recipe for pain and stress. Note: If you're feeling depressed and/or stressed, simply begin writing down everything in your life that you are thankful for and see what happens.

Advance Gratitude: Giving thanks now—in the present—for whatever you desire but that you have not yet achieved.[23]

Now gratitude is a good habit, and gratitude alone will improve your life. Advance gratitude, given in the present, is a necessary fundamental for fulfilling your desires. Why? Because advance gratitude sends a message to the conscious energy field that you are serious about achieving a given desire. You are so confident in the collaboration of the universe and its corroboration by manifestation that you are thanking the universe in advance for the fact that your desire has already been achieved. Advance gratitude exhibits total confidence and expectation! You are speaking the *Invisible Architect*'s language!

Say, for example, that your kids have a dirty or messy room. You could thank them as is normal *after* they finally have cleaned it up (this would be "now gratitude"), which will reinforce their good behavior. Or you could affirm that their room is organized and clean and thank them in

---

[23]"Having gratitude for something before you receive it is the secret catalyst to Spiritual manifesting" —Robert Collier, "Secrets to Spiritual Abundance"

advance for cleaning their room even though they haven't done it yet! They may look at you puzzled. But they may get the hint and just do it anyway. The *Invisible Architect* operates similarly but with more urgency and power. When it hears real and meaningful advance gratitude, the Architect knows you're serious, as you have spoken the Word with total certainty! Since the Word is Spiritual Law, it has no choice but to get busy carrying out your clear desire—that's the Law! [24] This is a personification, of course, but close to describing the actual spiritual mechanics at play from my experience.

I used to train German shepherds. Whenever I wanted to teach a new behavior, I would show the dog the behavior by modeling the behavior for and with the dog. I would then immediately reward and thank the dog by saying "good boy!" He'd look at me in a funny way because *he* didn't do the behavior. I did it for him! Example: If I wanted the dog to sit, I'd give him the "sit" command and then gently push his rear end down. I would thank and reward him. After a few repetitions, he'd connect the dots and realize that the audio command "sit" meant that he should put his back end down and he would get praise and a reward. This process works very well. But check this out: Sometimes, I'd walk up to my shepherd (his name was Odin) and out of the blue I'd say, "Good boy, Odin, good boy," and he'd get excited as hell and just sit down, and then I'd reward him yet again! Amazing, huh? You get the advance gratitude analogy? Just by showing gratitude as if the required action had already happened, my dog would carry out that action.

Nothing begins manifesting until your subconscious accepts your desire. Your tomato seed must be planted in your garden and nurtured before it will begin to grow. You need to sell your desire to your *heart and soul*— the *Invisible Architect*! Why the spiritual mechanics appear to be set up this

---

[24] "God is Word, God is Law, God is Spirit. The Word of God means the power of spirit to declare Itself into manifestation. The starting point of all creation is the WORD. The Word is the Concept, Idea, Image, or thought. God, the Architect, speaks and it is done!" —Ernest Holmes, "The Science of Mind"

way I don't know, but I think it is a brilliant process, given the lessons learned in the process of manifesting your desires!

A personification of this process might be as follows. The *Invisible Architect* receives your mental image as a desire through your subconscious mind. To the degree that your desire is clear, detailed, and has 100 percent certainty, that is the degree to which the *Invisible Architect* accepts your desire as Word and carries it out.[25]

If it is unclear and uncertain, the desire is difficult to discern and carry out. Imagine getting into a taxi in New York City. The taxi driver says, "Where to?" You say, "I don't know." Or you say, "Times Square." The taxi driver pulls away and you say, "Wait a minute. How about Wall Street? No, I'm not sure if I feel good—maybe I should go back to the hotel." Without a clear destination, spoken with certainty, the likelihood of arrival is doubtful—or even the likelihood of pulling away from the curb. The taxicab driver will probably throw you out of the taxi!

So, if your desire is clearly stated as already achieved and you have expressed advance gratitude, the *Invisible Architect* will think you are serious, accept your desire (i.e., command), and get to work using all of its power—powers beyond your comprehension and abilities—to reorganize the quantum energy in such a manner as to start the process of your wish being fulfilled. You must BE *there*, meaning *being* in the state of your desire having been fulfilled—as only then will your subjective experience (which you are vividly imagining with expectation) be realized objectively.

If your stated desire is not clear, however, and it is constantly changing, or it is confusing, or if doubt is mixed in with your desire, as well as other lower frequency emotions, then the *Invisible Architect*, like the taxicab driver, can't really act and do its job efficiently. As a matter of fact, it's worse than that! Whereas the taxicab driver will probably throw

---

[25] "In the beginning was the Word, and the Word was with God, and the Word was God." John 1:1.

you out of his cab if your directions are confusing, the *Invisible Architect* will carry out your exact desire in a manner that is confusing and disorganized, without any pushback. It's not there to evaluate your desires; there is what I call the law of self-determinism. The *Invisible Architect* is neutral.

Alert: So be careful and clear with your thoughts, or you will manifest all kinds of unwanted situations that can make your life non-optimal!

Imagine you and the willing taxicab driver are driving all over the Big Apple, never arriving anywhere! Welcome to the chaos and frustration of most people's lives. They don't understand the spiritual mechanics in the sphere of personal spiritual growth and having control over their thoughts—more on this topic later.

Here's a personification of the *Invisible Architect*. In *Conversations with God*, Neale Donald Walsch says that God has a one-word answer to all our communications, and that is "yes"! For example, if you think clearly and with certainty—a big mistake in this case— "I will *never* ever be able to afford to pay for my son's college education." The Quantum Energy Field (God) mirrors your clear thought back: "Yes, you'll *never* be able to afford to pay for your son's college education," and so you get exactly your stated desire. This is important! The Law of Attraction, the Law of Cause and Effect, is always in play. So, you need to police your thoughts, clearing them of unwanted desires (i.e., causes). Then *clearly* state them in the sequence above. BE is the stated desire. DO is to imagine the desire achieved (which will dictate short and long-term events), and HAVE involves expressing advance gratitude, which ensures motion toward your desire. Now there's one other fundamental that enters this equation, and that is *feeling* and *emotion*, which translates into *sincerity*!

Say a loved one had cancer and your goal was for that loved one to be cured. What would your feelings and emotions be if that happened—Oh my God, the battle is over! How thankful would you be? Wouldn't you be so excited that you couldn't sleep? Who would you tell the good news to? How would your loved one's life be different? How would your life be different? What emotions would you all be experiencing? In other words, what would you BE, DO, and HAVE in this case? What would you be feeling, doing, and experiencing because of this desire being achieved?

To imagine is to create your mental archetype in the thought universe. When you imagine your desire fulfilled, how does your life look in all areas? Give advance gratitude as if you had achieved your desire. Advance gratitude is like *mental time travel*. You go into the future and imagine (feel and perceive) what the *desire achieved* would be like. Then you travel back into the now, the present time, while carrying that feeling and excitement with you until it becomes so real that you have auto-hypnotized yourself. The desire *has* happened—it is not just that it will happen, but rather that it *has* happened! As discussed earlier, this state could be described as "remembering the future"[26] that you just imagined with your imagination. You are BEING your future self in the *now*. At that point, it becomes easy to have advance gratitude in the now because the desire *feels* like it indeed has already happened! And it has already happened in the Quantum Energy Field where all things already exist. The *future self* is the electromagnetic signature, which you are now BEING. This point of attraction begins reorganizing the All-energy Quantum Field and thus begins the miraculous manifestation (Law of Attraction) process of the *Invisible Architect*!

My take on why *feelings* and *emotions* are key to manifestation is that a) they amplify the power of your desire and b) they are the language that the *Invisible Architect* understands. They let the Architect know you are sincere and heartfelt about your desire rather than being just cautiously hopeful or even doubtful.

To keep your frequency high and the process in motion, use repetitive affirmations. For example, if health is your desire, repeat *I am healthy* until you are conscious only of your desired state: health. In other

---

[26] "The key is remembering the future."—Dr Joe Dispenza, *Becoming Supernatural*

words, you can't even remember (nor are you conscious of) your current undesirable circumstances. You are not aware of them anymore because you are only aware of your desired state. Repeating your affirmation is especially effective while in the hypnagogic state; this is the awareness state right before falling asleep. Now, acknowledge the Divine all-perfect power within you and be your new future self in the present! Raise your energy signature to its zenith and feel gratitude, appreciation, and thankfulness.

At this point the unified conscious energy field is 100 percent certain of your desire, and, to that degree, it accepts your desire just as fertile soil accepts an apple seed and immediately begins growing apples! The *reorganization* of the quantum energy has begun; this energy field is where all frequencies *already* exist concerning your desire. Enjoy the journey and have patience.

And, since you now taste victory, your supportive actions become clear and supercharged, which increases your activity and amplifies momentum!

Everything Is Energy!

Q&A Cognition 8

1. Q: What is a definition of faith?
   A: Believing passionately in something that does not yet exist. The nonexistent is whatever we have not sufficiently desired.

2. Q: If something in your life is non-optimal, how can you change it?
   A: Use the Be-Do-Have formula. First, change your mindset (BE); then change what you're doing (DO). Your non-optimal situation (HAVE) will then begin changing as your mindset and activities move toward your desire.

3. Q: What is the manifestation process?
   A: The process has three steps: BE, DO, and HAVE. BE is your Desire. Write it down as a completed statement. DO is the imagination. Use it to imagine (or create) your desire as already having been achieved. Your actions will follow accordingly while the *Invisible Architect* works its magic! HAVE is Gratitude. Give thanks now in the present for your desire being achieved.

4. Q: Where do our desires come from?
   A: Most likely our desires come from the *Invisible Architect*, who is speaking through you. So, don't ignore desires that are positive and constructive.

5. Q: What is a goal redefined?
   A: A goal restated as completed. For example, "I wish my migraines to be healed" would be changed to "My migraines are healed!"

6. Q: What is the role of the imagination in manifestation?
   A: Your mind can create any desire from your personal thought universe. Since everything is energy and all desires already exist as "unorganized potential energies and frequencies" waiting to

be organized into your desired reality, imagination begins and completes the manifestation process.

7. Q: What is advance gratitude?
   A: Advance gratitude is to give thanks in the present for a desire you wish to achieve in the future even though it is not yet achieved. It sends a message to the *Invisible Architect* that you have 100 percent faith and, indeed, expect the desire to be achieved!

8. Q: Why does your desire have to be clearly stated as already achieved?
   A: Because the *Invisible Architect* then accepts your clear desire and gets to work, using all its powers to reorganize quantum energy and to attract circumstances for realizing its fulfillment. If the desire is not clear, the Architect cannot act and do its job efficiently (as illustrated by the taxicab analogy).

9. Q: What is the purpose of an affirmation?
   A: Repetitively stating your desires as already completed keeps your frequency high, at the God-Frequency, and the manifestation process in progress! These affirmations are even more effective when you are in the hypnagogic state.

10. Write down several goals and redefine them as discussed into an affirmation. Then every night before retiring, state these affirmations repetitively and thank the Architect for helping you achieve them! Note: Best to do one at a time so you can focus.

Next Cognition…

Cognition 9
Prayer Understood

"Prayer—the world's greatest wireless connection."

—*Cornerstone Christian Ministries*

"Prayer is man's greatest power."

—*W. Clement Stone*

When I was growing up in the Catholic school system, I thought prayer was to simply rattle off a Hail Mary, recite an Our Father, say a rosary, or, when I needed something, ask God for help, and promise if I received whatever I needed, I would be a good boy! I had no clue—and in hindsight neither did my parents or teachers—of what real prayer was.

To be honest, I didn't really understand what prayer was until my late wife died of an aggressive cancer as I mentioned earlier. That was an awakening for me, the beginning of a new life, a rebirth. I began researching many authors, books, and subjects (see below) because after her tragic death, I was hungry for explanations about life!

I began reading and researching the following...

- After-death communications (ADCs).
- Out-of-body experiences and techniques (OBEs).
- New Thought movement & authors: New Thought is a set of beliefs concerning metaphysics, spiritual origins, affirmations, the discussion of how thoughts create reality, the subconscious and conscious mind, the Law of Attraction, spiritual healing, the life force, creative visualization, telepathy, how one's inner world creates their outer world, etc. (My favorite author was and still is Charles Haanel and his Master Key System.).
- Theosophy, spiritualism, psychic phenomena, hermeticism, mediumship, etc.
- The *Tibetan Book of the Dead* and the Bardo State, which assists a deceased being through death and to a favorable rebirth.
- The *Egyptian Book of the Dead*: Its two hundred chapters are a thrilling insight into beliefs about the trials, joys, and fears on the journey into death's mysterious realm.
- The Bible and Jesus' teachings, which I now had more respect for given my life-changing experiences and better mindset.
- Many past and current "-isms" and "-ologies," too numerous to mention.

I must have read over a hundred books on these subjects and took many courses, one of the best being The Master Key Experience by Mark Januszewski.

Before my wife died, we had an agreement that she would try and keep in touch with me from the "other side," and vice versa. It became an obsession as her fight with cancer and ultimate death was both horrific and at the same time spiritually life-changing for the both of us! I became so adamant about staying in contact with her and researching ADCs and what happens when we die, etc., that it led to my writing a book on the subject entitled *The Song That Never Ended*. The premise of the book was autobiographical about how we both met, fell in love, created music together, and then our fight with cancer, her apparent death, and then our post-death communications. I even corroborated these ADCs during many sessions with famous mediums, where my wife, under controlled conditions, came through and communicated to me.

My conclusion was 100 percent confirmation that we indeed are immortal spiritual beings and our *songs never end*! That's why I said "apparent" death—we don't die! (Suggested reading: *We Don't Die* by George Anderson)

Then if this wasn't amazing enough, something incredible happened! If you recall, I mentioned that during my teens I experienced flying around my neighborhood when I fell asleep. Later I determined these episodes weren't dreams at all but actual out-of-body occurrences or astral projections. But after my wife died, I was wondering why I couldn't easily fly around outside of my body anymore. So, I began reading many books on OBE techniques—the two most influential for me being...

1. *Adventures in the Afterlife* by William Buhlman
2. *Astral Dynamics: The Complete Book of Out of Body Experiences* by Robert Bruce

I tried every night, as I wanted to see if I could astral project and maybe meet up with my late wife, but to no avail. I was exhausted from not sleeping very well, but then one night, the following happened:

I was trying one of the many techniques I had been practicing, specifically "the roll out of bed" technique. This is a method of inducing an out-of-body experience while in bed or in a reclining position. It is effective because the act of rolling out of your bed is something that we each may experience many times a night, and the familiarity of this action makes it easy to visualize for the purpose of helping induce an out-of-body experience. I was in the hypnagogic state, very relaxed, and was affirming repeatedly "body sleep mind awake," which is the goal— allow the body to fall asleep but your mental awareness to remain awake. I was about to give up and was close to falling asleep and felt that maybe I needed to go to the bathroom, so I did the usual and rolled to the right. My feet landed on the floor as usual, but I felt unusually light and began levitating a little. I turned to my left and saw my body as clear as could be! I thought, *Wow! I'm out, and there is my body sleeping away on its side.* I affirmed "clarity now," a trick I had read about that focuses your out-of-body real-time vision. It worked! I felt totally aware and lucid, and so I decided to explore my immediate real time environment versus projecting into another dimension like I had read about.

I looked at the cable box and noted the exact time as being 3:34 a.m. to confirm I was not dreaming. I looked at the *subtle energy body* that my awareness had apparently downloaded into and walked over to the bedroom door, which was closed. I thought to myself that I should be able to pass this *subtle energy body* through the door, and so I reached out my hand and put it flat on the door. At first it felt kind of solid as usual, and I thought, *No, this isn't supposed to be,* and immediately my hand went through the door, and my energy body went with it. It was a fantastic but strange feeling, as if my molecular structure meshed with the molecular structure of the door until I pushed through and came out on the other side. *Everything indeed is energy,* I thought.

My German shepherd Odin, who sleeps in the hallway, turned around and looked right at me and initially freaked out, as he apparently saw or sensed his master coming through the door! He then calmed down, and I continued my real time environment explorations. I went outside, easily levitated at will, and flew around the neighborhood as I did when I was a kid until I felt a pull, and then in an instant I was back in my body totally awake. I had studied that unless you immediately write down the incident, it might not download to your standard memory banks, and you'll have no memory of the incident having happened if you fall back asleep.[27]

Not only was this very incredible and therapeutic, but it totally proved to me that indeed I was a separate spiritual being whose awareness could somehow live on without a body. I also now knew for sure that my late

---

[27] We all naturally have frequent nightly out-of-body episodes but don't easily remember them without awareness practice.

wife was okay. I went back to sleep with a smile on my face and awakened totally rejuvenated spiritually, mentally, and physically. It was not long after that the *Invisible Architect* sent my angelic soulmate to me as discussed earlier, and I was able to put my attention back on this side, but with my new soulmate!

But if you're wondering if I continued my out-of-body explorations and rendezvoused with my late wife, the answer is yes! I had many rendezvous, which were not only refreshing but also proved conclusively to me that death is a dimensional transition, and our unique energy signatures continue—our *songs indeed never end*! This wonderful realization allowed each of us to move on with our lives—her on the other side (dimension) and me on this side. So, instead of being obsessed with her and the other side and what happens after death, she urged me to reorient to my present life, which I did. It was closure and a relief! I began life anew with my new angelic soulmate Barbara Novello—it was a miracle! So then...back to prayer.

What is an effective way to pray to get results? Surely, I thought, there can't be some separate almighty being somewhere that created the universe and for amusement answers prayers at random and creates good and bad and allows evil? My experiences and observations say otherwise. They say that there is indeed a Quantum Intelligent Energy that permeates everything, including us, and that not only are we all ONE—everything is energy—but that once we become conscious(aware) of this ONENESS with this Universal Good, beliefs in all things negative—evil, limitation, sickness, death, poverty—can no longer exist unless you decide so and/or allow them to. We create and co-create these things through our ignorance of spiritual mechanics; but therein lies *self-determinism*, which is the freedom of the game of life.

This is the answer then why some of our desires (prayers) are answered and some not. If we believe and are conscious of a being separate from this Universal Intelligent Energy, then how can our prayers be fulfilled (answered)? But on the other hand, if we are conscious of our oneness with this Intelligent Energy, that we are of the same nature, then sure your prayers must be answered (fulfilled)—it is a Spiritual Law.[28]

There is a designer, a *dream weaver*, within each of us, awaiting our recognition (conscious awareness of). Once recognized, it takes our wishes, desires, dreams, thoughts, and beliefs, no matter how small or big, good or bad, and manifests them in the "garden of reality" proportionate to our focus, expectations, and faith. We can imagine a life of abundance, harmony, love, and inspiration or one of lack, chaos, hate, and degradation. Although at times it may seem otherwise, we have total choice or self-determinism. A fertile garden cares not what seed is planted. It immediately goes to work giving birth to that seed's purpose; e.g., a tomato seed grows only into a tomato, a weed into a weed, etc. The soil cares not, but the farmer—the planter of the seed—should, and that is you and me.

So, what is prayer? I've read that…

"Prayer is when you talk to God, meditation is when you listen to God."

—Ronald Roberts

One might say that *prayer* then is talking with the Intelligent Energy Field. *Focused prayer* is clearly asking the Intelligent Energy Field that permeates all things to express itself through you. Since the *Invisible Architect* is all-good, all-knowing, all-love, all-perfect, and within each of us, then your desire clearly stated and imagined as already been delivered to you, thereby prompting your "advance gratitude", must manifest. It has no choice; it is the Law!

Remember the Be-Do-Have sequence?

BE is your wish clearly stated. DO is you imagining what your life would be like when the wish is fulfilled, which if done correctly and consistently, activates the Architect's reorganization of the quantum energy field—the manifestation process—thereby triggering your feelings. DO is also any action you undertake to speed up and amplify

---

[28]"And whatsoever you shall ask in my name, that will I do."—John 14:13

the manifestation, which if you pay attention to your inner voice, will come naturally to you. Trust me; once you become expert at using your imagination, your *feelings* will be so strong that they will lead you to obsessive and excited activity toward getting your wish fulfilled! HAVE is the exact same gratitude you would express when your desire has been fulfilled but expressing it in the now, the present, versus expressing it later when it manifests in the Physical Universe.

Example: If you are poor, your desire might be to BE wealthy. So, state that clearly in your focused prayer. Then begin to act and feel you are wealthy and prosperous and able to DO everything that abundance would permit. Envelope yourself in this feeling! As you continue to repeat this process of *feeling* wealthy—I am wealthy and prosperous— you will soon begin to forget about lack and poverty and all its problems and begin gradually assuming the *persona* of a wealthy person in your *personal thought universe*. The manifestation process has begun. At this point give thanks that your desire has manifested in *your* personal universe and soon, unless acted upon by counter-thoughts such as "I'll never probably be wealthy," "This isn't working," "I knew it wouldn't work," "My Dad said I wouldn't amount to anything," etc., wealth will manifest in the reality universe, the universe of your physical senses— the Physical Universe.

The following Be-Do-Have similarity scale might help understanding.

Be	Do	Have
Subjective	Imagination	Objective
Desire	Feeling of Wish Fulfilled	Gratitude
Inner World	Creates	Outer World
Beingness	Doingness	Havingness
Cause	Action	Effect
Begin	Continue	Achieve
Thought	Manifestation Process	Reality
Strategy	Execution	Success

Summary

Everything is composed of energy. Thought is a form of energy. Focused thought or prayer possesses the innate ability to influence, restructure, and ultimately mold energy into its correspondent manifestation.

Thought works on different subject planes. For example, one who is thinking on the thought plane of wealth is inspired with an idea of success, and it could not be otherwise. He is thinking on the success plane, and as like attracts like, his thoughts attract other similar thoughts, all of which contribute to his success. His receiver is attuned for success thoughts only. All other messages fail to reach his consciousness; hence, he knows nothing of them. His antennae, as it were, reach into the Universal Ether (Intelligent Energy Field) and connect with the ideas by which his plans and ambitions may be realized.

Drill: Select a subject with which you are familiar. Begin to think thoughts about that subject. Notice that soon other similar thoughts and ideas will follow each other in rapid succession. One thought will suggest another, etc. You will soon be surprised at some of the thoughts that have made you a channel of their manifestation. Why? Because everything exists in the Quantum Field as *unorganized energy* awaiting organization from the observer's thoughts and intentions. The intelligent conscious energy detects your clear thoughts about being a success coach, author, and motivational speaker, and the faucet is opened! Just pay attention and pick and choose the thoughts and ideas that come your way like magic! Enjoy the show, but don't forget to be proactive and act (DO).

This Law of Attraction is neither good nor evil, neither moral nor immoral; it is a neutral law that always flows in conjunction with the desires of the individual. This is called Spiritual Magnetism! If you put your attention on worry, lack, and failure, for example, well…it will deliver more of the same, and there goes a dwindling spiral that can fool you into thinking you're doomed, you're unlucky, "why me", etc., when in fact you are simply ignorant of the spiritual mechanics and using them incorrectly and inefficiently. For example, electricity understood and used correctly has been a miraculous human utility, but used incorrectly it can cause fires and electrocute you! Same with fire, nuclear energy, guns, automobiles, medicine, etc.

Cause and effect are mirror correspondents of each other. Cause A manifests Effect A, and Effect A is caused by Cause A, not B or C or X! And another factor is universe or energy-field density. The less dense the energy environment, the faster the restructuring of the Energy Field by the *Invisible Architect* to accomplish manifestation. The denser the energy environment, the slower the restructuring of the Energy Field by the *Invisible Architect*. Therefore, manifestation takes *time* according to the complexity of the desire in the Physical Universe. In the thought universe, for example, you can imagine anything, anything at all. For example, imagine a blue elephant sitting on top of the Empire State Building, and it will appear instantly, right? But try that in the Physical Universe and see what happens. It's much more difficult; why? Well, the Physical Universe is composed of low, coarse frequencies, and so, although I suppose it's possible, it would take great planning and effort to put an elephant on top of the Empire State Building.

To review and summarize: The effectiveness and speed that your thought restructures an energy environment is determined by the *intensity* of the thought and the *density* of the energy upon which it is acting on. In the manifest Physical Universe, your thoughts and corresponding feelings and gratitude normally don't materialize instantly as they do in your personal thought universe. That's why you must have patience. Due to the low frequency and density of the Physical Universe, there is usually a time lag before manifestation…and a good thing, as if there wasn't, what kind of game would that be? Instantaneous manifestation may sound good, but that would set up a scary situation, as unless you had absolute total control of your thoughts, imagine the chaos if all your thoughts and desires instantly manifested—yikes! However this game got created, it was well-thought-out, pure genius, and yet another proof of intelligence creating us versus some kind of random accident!

Therefore, don't entertain thoughts or statements that you don't desire to come true (manifest). If you do, use thought substitution, substituting positive opposite thoughts in their place ASAP! More on this later...

Why? Because all thoughts, statements, and beliefs that are created or agreed with and that become predominant lead to more of the same, as per like frequencies attract like frequencies. They influence similar thoughts, statements, and beliefs that lead to decisions and actions supportive of the current predominant thoughts and beliefs that manifest similar realities. So, even though our thoughts and beliefs luckily don't manifest instantly, they still begin the *process* instantly, thereby heading you eventually into an undesirable reality, usually unknowingly. If you're going to change your outer reality, then change it into something desirable. Make sense? And do it quickly!

Be careful, therefore, as your focused prayer is a spiritual transaction with the *Invisible Architect*.

Morning Prayer:

"Pick me up, Invisible Architect, and hold me in Your loving arms. Protect me from the challenges of the day and remove the heaviness from my heart. Inspire me with the knowledge that You and I can handle anything!"

Q&A Cognition 9

1. Q: What is prayer?
   A: Prayer is talking with the Intelligent Energy Field—the *Invisible Architect*. It is clearly asking the *Invisible Architect* that permeates all things to express itself through you and manifest your desires.

2. Q: What is the nature of focused thought?
   A: Focused thought (prayer) possesses the innate ability to influence, restructure, and ultimately mold the energy from the Intelligent Energy Field into its corresponding manifestation.

3. Select a subject that you are familiar with and begin to think about that subject. Notice the thoughts that begin manifesting that are making you a channel of their manifesting. Pay attention to these thoughts, pick and choose the ones that come your way, and act as you wish!

4. Q: What does it mean that the Law of Attraction is neutral?
   A: It is a neutral law that always flows in conjunction with your desires, whether good, bad, moral, or immoral.

5. Q: What is Spiritual Magnetism?
   A: Whatever you put your attention (thought energy) on, you will attract more of the same. If you put it on negative energy, you get more of the same; on positive energy, you get more of the same. Advice: Be careful what you put your attention on!

6. Q: What is meant by the statement "The effectiveness and speed which thought restructures and energy environment is determined by the intensity of the thought and the density of the energy which it is acting on"?
   A: Given the frequency density of the Physical Universe, your thoughts and corresponding feelings normally don't materialize instantly as they do in your less dense personal thought universe.

7. Q: Why is it important to not entertain thoughts that you don't wish to come true (manifest)?
    A: Because all thoughts that are created by you from within or agree with those that come from without and that become predominant, lead to more of the same, per the datum "like frequencies attract like frequencies."

Next Cognition…

Cognition 10
Your Life Blueprint

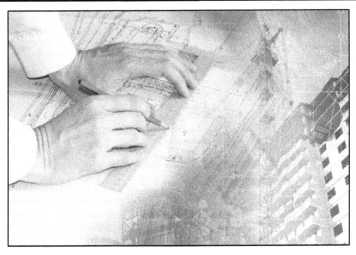

"Success is neither magical nor mysterious. Success is the natural consequence of consistently applying basic fundamentals."

—*Jim Rohn*

"The only way by which we may secure possession of power is to become conscious of power, and we can never become conscious of power until we learn that all power is from within."

—*Charles Haanel*

Question: What does it take to manifest (construct), for example, a building in the Physical Universe?
Answer: A clear and accurate blueprint design and its supervised competent construction until completion.

Well, you are your Life Architect! You are the one responsible for creating your "Life Blueprint" and for supervising its construction until completion! Imagine the frustration and chaos created from having no blueprint, an inaccurate blueprint, a constantly changing blueprint, a contradictory blueprint, somebody else's blueprint, etc.

In the case of a building, wouldn't you want it designed and built by the best architect and professional builders who use the best materials and who follow the exact agreed-upon blueprint?

You are the Chief Architect of your life, so you must first create an accurate blueprint and then hire a top professional to carry it out. And guess who that top professional should be?

Your own personal *Invisible Architect*, who is accessed through your subconscious mind.

What good is writing down your life blueprint if you don't have the wherewithal to complete it? If you hired an architect to design your dream home, then what? You must still hire a construction crew to carry out the plans, right?

Same goes for your life blueprint.

First, you must research and create your exact blueprint because without this, you are a pilot without a flight plan! You can't take off without a flight plan, and if you do, where would you go, etc.?

Note: If you don't know what your life's purpose is, you need to spend some quality time figuring it out.

Here are a few tips:

- What drives you?
- Do you have any natural skills or talents?
- If you were independently wealthy and money was not an issue, what would you do?
- Is there any charity or worthy cause you'd like to further?
- Is there a person or group you'd like to help?

Remember, your life's purpose doesn't have to be huge, like solving world hunger. It could involve hairstyling and making people look good! Or fixing car engines. Or helping the elderly. Or playing a musical instrument, etc. And yes, there's nothing wrong with wanting to be a billionaire so that you can be more effective at whatever you choose to do!

There are many books on the subject, so read and research and listen carefully to your inner voice—the *Invisible Architect*. If you ask the *Invisible Architect*, pay attention. You *will* get your answer.[29]

Once you choose a desire to manifest—whether it be small or large— the Law of Attraction is quite simple. All you need to do is just plant the desire (seed) into your subconscious garden, imagine you have already achieved it until you have convinced yourself that you have (auto-hypnosis), and then *feel* it in your heart! Give advance thanks for the desire being fulfilled...that's it! Have patience!

Just as you expect a tomato seed to turn into a tomato eventually, so you must expect your seed of desire to turn into itself. A tomato seed cannot become a potato; it can only become itself, and if it isn't fussed with, dug up to see if it's growing, eaten by some animals, or denied its nutrients, it will turn into a tomato plant. Same goes with your desire. Plant it daily into your subconscious through repetitive affirmations, especially while you're in the hypnagogic state, and don't fuss. Believe and expect it to take root; the *Invisible Architect* will get to work, reorganizing the Quantum Intelligent Energy Field, and your desire will begin to grow as long as you don't plant countering thoughts, beliefs, or desires (e.g., "this will never work," "I'll never be affluent," "I've always had trouble with having money," "it's been three months, and I'm still broke," etc.).

Also, never use time as a measurement of success and never consult reality. We're changing reality, not observing, validating, and/or agreeing with it; this is a big difference! To change an undesirable outer reality, you must first change your inner reality. Think, "I am affluent, "or if that is too hard to confront, "I am becoming more and more affluent every day!" Once you experience the concept of your inner reality, you

---

[29] If you want assistance in discovering your Definite Major Purpose, I highly recommend The Master Key Experience. For more information, go to masterkeyexperience.com, and say I sent you!

will see that it creates your outer reality, and you can then state the goal has been completed, which is best!

However, just because the Law of Cause and Effect is simple—i.e., thoughts ultimately create our desired reality—it does not necessarily mean it's easy to get results from it. Johann Sebastian Bach, for instance, said, "It's easy to play any musical instrument. All you have to do is touch the right key at the right time, and the instrument will play itself!"

This is correct! As a musician, I have experience with this. However, that simple process can take many years of patience and dedicated practice, studying and applying the fundamentals. When we see a great pianist effortlessly perform even the most difficult of compositions, we marvel. However, if we witnessed the dedication and work involved, we'd be even more impressed.

The same applies to learning the spiritual mechanics of the Law of Cause and Effect and our interacting with the *Invisible Architect*. There are fundamentals that need to be understood and applied correctly to produce the desired results. And therein lies the reason why many have difficulty with it and incorrectly assume it doesn't work!

It works if you do the work and work it correctly. It is a law, the Law of Cause and Effect.

When it doesn't work as intended, there are reasons:

1. Ignorance of the spiritual mechanics involved.

2. Incorrect and inconsistent application of the fundamentals once learned.

Important Fundamentals

Note: By simply understanding the terms and fundamentals below, you will greatly improve your understanding of the spiritual mechanics of working with the *Invisible Architect* to design and manifest your life's blueprint.

Spiritual Mechanics: The relationship between the Universal Consciousness and its creations and the interactions thereof.

The *Invisible Architect*: God, THE Creator, Intelligent Energy, Quantum Field, Cosmic Conscious, First Cause, One Mind, Universal Mind, Over-Soul, Eternal Spirit, Inner Voice—THE Creator of everything!

Spiritual Being (You): The Being who is the individual separate from all things, including your body. Each of us is a unique version of the *Invisible Architect* attempting to express itself as a human being. We all have our own unique intelligent energy signature. This is the basis of self-determinism.

Human Being: Spirit, Mind, Body—A unique eternal energy signature that has a viewpoint and that can think and create. This organized intelligent energy (spirit) inhabits a body and uses an interface called the mind to control the body to achieve various desires. Humans come with their own personal *Invisible Architect*—a connection to the ONE Intelligent Universal Energy.

Human Body: The human body is essentially a living carbon/oxygen engine that runs on low-temperature combustion carbon fuel, somewhat like any internal-combustion engine. Like an automobile engine, a body takes in fuel, burns it, and expels the unburned part of the fuel as waste. This unique biological organization of flesh and blood vehicle is used by the spirit to express itself and be identified. It is not the being itself because when the body ceases to function, the spirit leaves. A miracle of Divine creation!

Be-Do-Have Sequence: What you ARE determines what you DO and what you will ultimately achieve (HAVE).

Thought: Energy forms created in the mind by you, the spirit, rather than the forms perceived through the senses—an instance of thinking. There are particles of energy all around you. These particles coalesce to create matter. Your thoughts are energy, your words are energy, and your actions are energy.

You create manifestations through thoughts, words, and actions that use energy to form objects, conditions, and experiences. The thought (desire) is instant and complete, but its manifestation is subject to the Law of Growth, which usually involves time, although in some cases can be almost instantaneous, depending on the nature of the desire and power and clarity of the thought. It is important to understand that the perfection of the desire is in the thought universe, but because we do not yet see that perfection in the manifest universe with our senses, it does not mean it is not in the process of manifesting. We can, however, facilitate this growth or evolutionary process by conscious cooperation with the *Invisible Architect*. We do this simply with the recognition of the *Intelligent Energy* within each of us. The creative action of the spirit then takes place through the laws of our thinking.[30]

Focused Prayer: A clear statement of your desire already achieved planted into your subconscious mind awaiting manifestation; your personal dialogue with God. Prayer is best done while in the hypnagogic state, for this is the time that the conscious and subconscious are creatively joined.

Hypnagogic State: The transitional state between wakefulness and sleep; the state of consciousness during the onset of sleep. Sleep is the natural door into the subconscious. It is in sleep and in prayer, a similar state, that we enter the subconscious to make our impressions to and receive our instructions from the *Invisible Architect*. This is the ideal time to plant your seed (desire) in your subconscious garden because the conscious mind is somewhat inactive and not likely to give you any pushback (counter-intention) to your desire. In other words, the garden is ready to accept your seed; the birds are sleeping, and no one is around to dig up your seed or eat it. If your seed is not planted correctly it won't be accepted and grow (manifest).

Brain Wave Frequencies: There are five distinct brain wave frequencies: namely Beta, Alpha, Theta, Delta, and the lesser-known Gamma. Understanding these frequencies and learning how to induce

---

[30]"The Divine ideal (desire) can only be externalized in our objective life in proportion as it is first formed in our thought. And it takes form in our thought only to the extent to which we apprehend its existence in the Divine Mind. By the nature of the relation between the universal mind and the individual mind, it is strictly a case of reflection; and in proportion as the mirror." —The Dore Lectures Thomas Troward

and control them opens you up to the world of your subconscious mind where you can design and achieve your lifestyle blueprint with exact precision.[31]

Beta (12-30Hz) is present in normal waking consciousness and is heightened during times of stress; the Alpha brain wave (7.5-14Hz) in deep relaxation; Theta (4-7.5Hz) in meditation and light sleep; and the slowest, Delta (0.5-4Hz), in deep dreamless sleep and transcendental meditation. The less recognized Gamma is fastest (above 40Hz) and associated with sudden insight. The optimal level for visualization is the Alpha-Theta border at 7-8Hz. It is the gateway to your subconscious mind.

- **Beta (12-30Hz):** Normal waking consciousness and a heightened state of alertness, logic, and critical reasoning.
- **Alpha (7.5-12Hz):** Associated with deep relaxation with the eyes usually closed and while daydreaming. Optimal for programming your mind for success, as Alpha frequencies heighten your imagination, visualization, memory, learning, and concentration. Alpha is the gateway to your subconscious mind.
- **Theta (4-7.5Hz):** Associated with deep meditation and light sleep, including the REM dream state. Theta is the realm of your subconscious mind. It is also known as the twilight or hypnagogic state, as it is normally only momentarily experienced as you drift off to sleep (from Alpha) and arise from deep sleep (from Delta). A sense of deep spiritual connection and oneness with the Universe can be experienced at Theta. Vivid visualizations, great inspiration, profound creativity, exceptional insight, as well as your mind's most deep-seated programs, are all at Theta.
- **Delta (0.5-4Hz):** The slowest frequency, present in deep, dreamless sleep and in very deep, transcendental meditation where awareness is completely detached. Delta is the gateway to the Universal Mind and the Collective Intelligence whereby

---

[31]*Mind Your Reality* by Tania Kotsos. Brain wave frequencies taken from this author's writings.

information received is otherwise unavailable at the conscious level. Delta is associated with deep healing and regeneration, underlining the importance of deep sleep to the healing process.

- **Gamma (30-100Hz):** The most recently discovered range. This is the fastest in frequency at above 40Hz (some researchers do not distinguish Beta from Gamma waves). Although little is known about this state of mind, initial research shows Gamma waves are associated with bursts of insight and high-level information processing.

Universal Mind: One Mind, Three Functions

- **The Universal Mind:** THE Creative Intelligence, the Quantum Energy Field that permeates everything—the *Invisible Architect!*
- **Conscious Universal Mind:** Your objective or thinking mind given to you by the Creator that uses your senses to perceive and analyze. It is the interface between you and your subconscious or subjective mind and Quantum Field. There are five basic senses but many others as well, such as balance, movement, body awareness, heat and cold sense, pain, hunger, mental stress, gravity, etc. The conscious universal mind has no memory and can only hold one thought at a time, which can be a good thing—see the Law of Thought Substitution below.
- **Subconscious Universal Mind:** Your subjective memory bank and unique personal servant that manages various bodily survival activities and carries out your conscious mind's instructions. It is the *Invisible Architect* expressing itself through you. It permanently stores everything that ever happens to you. It can not only store but also retrieve data, which is why hypnosis works if the person allows. [32] It is subjective. It does not think or reason independently. It merely obeys the commands it receives from your conscious mind. Together, if used correctly, your conscious and subconscious mind make a good support team.

---

[32] Hypnotism has its pluses and minuses and is not recommended, as you are giving control to an outside source that implants commands and suggestions—hence, a loss of self-determinism.

Your conscious mind under your supervision is the gardener who plants the seeds. Your subconscious mind can be thought of as the garden, or fertile soil, in which the seeds germinate and grow with the assistance from the *Invisible Architect*.

YOU are the spiritual being in charge—the one who gives the orders to the conscious mind (gardener). Your subconscious mind—your personalized *Invisible Architect*—is the fertile ground awaiting the growth of your desire.

Your subconscious mind is an unquestioning servant that creates your outer conscious world consistent with your emotionalized thoughts and predominant beliefs. It is neutral. It grows either flowers or weeds in the garden of your life. Whatever desire you plant is based on the mental equivalents you create. This is the Law of Correspondence or Cause and Effect.

Its job is to respond exactly the way you programmed it. Your personalized subconscious mind makes everything you say and do fit a pattern consistent with your self-concept. This is your master program. Changing your self-awareness or consciousness then instantly begins changing your personal reality—hint!

Example: If you are conscious of lack and limitation, sickness, stress, and struggle, or abundance or affluence, harmony, health, and love, well, then, that's what you create or attract. Hence the name Law of Attraction, which I think would be better named the Law of Correspondence.

Goal: "I wish my rheumatoid arthritis to be healed!" This is a goal not yet fulfilled, so by its very nature it has time involved. In fact, the process of creating a goal is an admittance of the goal as not yet achieved. It is therefore not as effective as a precise statement of your wish fulfilled or your goal redefined. In other words, this is the future collapsed into the present. Goals are nice to make and better than not having goals and therefore no future hope, but they are negative in a sense that they acknowledge that they've not been achieved yet. It is better to state or redefine any goal as having been completed in your thought universe, your mind, even though in the manifest universe of perceptions it has not been completed. Why? Because time is the enemy of manifestation. You want the wish fulfilled in the present, not in the future, which never can be reached.

Goal Redefined: "My rheumatoid arthritis is healed; I am healthy!" This is your future goal redefined, stated in the present having been fulfilled. When you plant this seed in the garden of reality—the Quantum Energy Field where all energy and potential creation already exists (as everything is energy)—the spiritual Architect immediately begins working on reorganizing energy and completing this desire as it is correctly stated in the present, the now, as having been achieved. If it is stated as a goal, the Intelligent Energy Field simply acknowledges your goal but doesn't get to work until you take the future out of it!

So, as a personification, if you state, "I want my rheumatoid arthritis healed," it simply says, "Okay, I get it. You want your arthritis healed. I hear you." But if you state, "My rheumatoid arthritis is healed; I am healthy," it reacts like, "Okay, his arthritis is healed! I better get to work to make that happen, as he clearly stated that is so. I'll use my unlimited knowledge and powers because if I don't, the head Invisible Architect will have my badge!" This is a humorous personification of the process, of course, but from my experience it gives you the modus operandi.

Imagination (Creative Visualization): Imagination is you practicing being God, the *Invisible Architect*! What did I just say? I said imagination is you practicing being the *Invisible Architect*! Why? Because it is the gateway to reality! Whatever you imagine (create) in your inner world will objectify in the manifest universe but only if you practice, understand, and apply the right spiritual mechanics. Imagination is so powerful that it cannot only assume the "feeling" of your desire fulfilled, it is also capable of incarnating the idea, too! Imagination is most likely how the *Invisible Architect* created the Universe in the beginning. "Believe that ye receive and ye shall receive" (Mark 11:24) is basically the same as "Imagine that you are, and you shall be." It's the Be-Do-Have sequence—most likely what caused the Big Bang or evolution or whatever happened that created this universe!

Now Gratitude: Giving thanks for everybody and everything in your life every day.

Advance Gratitude: Giving thanks for anything you *desire* as if it has already manifested in the Physical Objective Universe, even though it has only manifested in your personal subjective universe!

Law of Attraction: This is the last and most important step of the manifestation process: the ability to attract into our lives whatever we are focusing on; our predominant thoughts. It is the Law of Attraction which uses the power of the mind to translate whatever is in our thoughts and materialize them into reality. In basic terms, all thoughts turn into things eventually, that is if they remain pure and focused!

Exercise: Select a subject with which you are familiar. Begin to think about only that subject. After a short while, thoughts will follow each other in rapid succession. One thought will suggest another. You will soon be surprised at some of the thoughts that have made you a channel of their manifestation.

This Law of Attraction is neither good nor evil, neither moral nor immoral; it is a neutral law that transmits and receives frequencies in conjunction with the desires of the individual. This is called Spiritual Magnetism!

Law of Correspondence: We live in an infinite sea of *energy-mind-substance*. It is sensitive to the highest degree. It takes form according to the mental demand. Thought forms the environment from which the substance expresses. Our ideal vision is the mold from which our future will emerge. All things are the result of the thought process.

By concentration we have made the *connection* between the finite and the Infinite, the limited and the unlimited, the visible and the invisible, the personal and the impersonal.

Throughout the entire universe, the Law of Cause and Effect is ever at work. This law is supreme; here a cause, there an effect. They can never operate independently. One corresponds to the other. Therefore…to change any unwanted effect (condition in the outer world), one must change its cause (condition in the inner world)!

Law of Thought Substitution: In the mental or spiritual realm, the realm of thought, a thought you want to let go of must be replaced immediately by another thought. In other words, it is impossible to eliminate a thought from your mind unless you fill the "mental" space with something else or, with great discipline, have trained yourself to just be—*perceive with no thinking, evaluation, or effort!*

Just as in the physical realm, where no two objects can occupy the same place at the same time, it's the same in the mental realm. The reason for this is that you are forever thinking; you cannot *not* think about something. If you are thinking about something unpleasant, such as having to go through a tax audit, you cannot *not* think about it unless you replace it with another more comfortable thought. It could be "My tax audit went well" or a completely disrelated thought, such as "I love my new puppy!"

This is a much easier solution to handling unwanted thoughts than shutting off all thinking, which most say is almost impossible. Why? Because to achieve this, one would have to just BE and PERCEIVE. To master this ability in today's quick-fix society can take an entire lifetime! It is very difficult to do, and most fail. It takes much self-sacrifice, practice, and discipline in the form of prayer and meditation but nevertheless is possible. Although it has its benefits, it is not very practical in this predominantly action-universe to focus only on BE—at least not for most of us! This is a Be + Do = Have universe. Sure, it may give you relief from a "noisy" mind and reduce physical and emotional stress, which is a good thing, but it's only temporary, as you'll want to get back into the exciting game of manifesting your desires!

It would be more ideal to act and live life and handle stress naturally during the process of living. Wouldn't it be more constructive to just become skilled at controlling your thoughts in order to design a better life? I think so because living and operating in the physical dimension seems to be about learning how to manifest our desires, learning lessons in the process, and helping others do the same, thereby creating a better world, versus learning how to sit on a mountaintop and contemplating one's navel in order to achieve *nirvana*—a transcendent state in which there is neither suffering, desire, nor sense of self and that causes you to be released from the effects of karma and the cycle of death and rebirth! That's a different and worthwhile path but not the purpose of this book, which is about taking action and designing your life from within. Personally, I don't think the mind is programmed to *just* BE in the now. I think it is made to Be + Do = Have, which *is* the manifestation process.

The mind perceives the present, draws upon knowledge and experience from the past, time travels into the future to anticipate threats, evaluates progress toward goals, imagines the ideal, and much more! Besides, there is no such thing as a *fixed-present!* Trying to really achieve a perfect present is like trying to nail down water! It's more like an *ever-changing present*, which can never be captured. On the other hand, allowing your thought energy to be unknowingly fixed in the past or the future is equally counterproductive, as it steals the miracle of the present! Success, therefore, depends upon effortless mental time travel between the past, present, and future at the speed of thought while constantly making decisions that lead to actions and desires being fulfilled (Be + Do = Have)! This is the manifestation process.

Yes, "to be or not to be" is an important question, but only a third of the equation, the other two-thirds being the Do and Have.

So, maybe the more important question is:

To Be, Do, and Have or not to Be, Do, and Have?—that is the question.

Is it better to design and achieve your ideal life and help others do the same and make this a better place (as God knows, it needs help) or to spend a lifetime trying to achieve some sort of illusive state of personal enlightenment? Your choice, of course.

What are your thoughts?

Theory of Thought Substitution

Our minds, when awake, alternate between three states:

Awake states:

1. Negative Thoughts (Life in Reverse)
2. Positive Thoughts (Life in Drive)
3. No Thoughts (Life in Neutral)

The negative and positive thought states could be defined as kinetic (active) states and moving toward unhappiness or happiness, respectively, whereas the no thought state could be defined as a state of zero thought activity with potential for activity—a static state of just *being and perceiving* as regards to thinking.

Note: This is not to be confused with the sleep state—a condition of body and mind such as that which typically recurs for several hours every night, in which the nervous system is relatively inactive, the eyes closed, the postural muscles relaxed, and consciousness practically suspended. It is distinguished from wakefulness by a decreased ability to react to stimuli but it is more reactive than a coma or disorders of consciousness, with sleep displaying very different and active brain patterns.

Many of us are in reverse, with our energy predominantly focused on negative thoughts. These create negative emotions, which lead to destructive decisions and activities that manifest unwanted outer-world situations.

Some of us, however, are in drive, and our attention is focused on positive thoughts. These create positive, uplifting emotions, leading to constructive, pro-survival decisions and activities that move toward designing (manifesting) our outer world desires.

Be-Do-Have (Car Analogy):

Negative Thoughts (Reverse Gear) create Destructive Activities and Undesired Situations.
Positive Thoughts (Drive Gear) create Constructive Activities and Desired Situations.

And as mentioned earlier, very few have mastered, even if temporarily, the state of neutrality, meaning no thoughts, the state of pure beingness, zero desires, no activity, meditation, enlightenment—just being in the present or in the now, as described by authors such as Jon Kabat-Zinn (*Falling Awake*), Ram Dass (*Be Here, Now*), and Eckhart Tolle (*The Power of Now*).

So, short of entering at will the state of *pure being* in times of need, which in reality most fail at, the next best and most practical solution is to apply the Law of Thought Substitution and quickly substitute positive thoughts in place of negative thoughts and continue on with the game of life—Be-Do-Have activity. This is much more practical and easier to succeed at—more on this in the next Cognition.

Postulate: To assume or claim as true; affirm. To affirm, ask, demand; to declare as true.

Exercise: Try postulating "I just am" repetitively when your mind seems fixated on a negative thought and see what happens.

Law of Opposites: You'll know if you're on the right track with manifesting your desires if you begin to get major pushback, challenges, failures, struggles, etc. Why? Because to be conscious of success, you must be aware of its opposite: failure; otherwise, there's no conscious point of view reference.

Therefore…

1. Your failures contain the seeds of success.
2. Your success contains the seeds of failure.
3. It is, however, your choice.

Affirm (postulate) and then let go and believe in your heart what you desire is manifesting. As you begin experiencing the pushback, the apparent failure, use that as a sign that the universe is reorganizing and manifesting. All hell may be breaking loose, but continue, as this is the *Invisible Architect* at work reorganizing your life and dynamics! Smile and continue the process toward the ideal. Where your mind goes, energy flows. Let go!

If you put your attention on the opposite negative unwanted reality—any pushback that you observe and/or are experiencing—you will slow and possibly sabotage the manifestation in progress that you're not even aware is occurring. This is a major reason why many fail at applying the Law of Attraction.

Law of Success: Service; that we get what we give. For this reason, we should consider it a great privilege to be able to give. Success is an effect, not a cause. If we wish to achieve any effect, we must determine the cause—or idea, belief, or thought—that created the effect.

Law of Giving: A simple law: If you want joy, give joy; if love is what you seek, offer love; if you crave material affluence, help others become prosperous; if you desire more money, give money feely.

Affirmations: Short, positive statements spoken aloud or as thoughts that describe a desired situation, habit, or goal. They are stated as facts in the present that have been already completed. Example: "I have a lavish, dependable income." Repeating these statements frequently, especially in a meditative or hypnagogic state, impresses them into your subconscious until accepted. This triggers the *Invisible Architect* into action to corroborate the desire's fruition into your life. It also attracts like thoughts, beliefs, and decisions in your life, which lead to actions that further support the manifestation process.

Remember, the *Invisible Architect* has unlimited powers to make these positive statements a reality. In other words, to make your BE become your HAVE! Beware of counter-affirmations, as they can slow down or prevent the original affirmation (stated desire) from manifesting. Example: "Who am I kidding…I'll probably never have a great income."

In summary, to begin designing your desired life, do the following:

1. Manifestation: "Where your mind goes, energy flows" (Ernest Holmes, *The Science of Mind*)
2. "Thought + Feeling = Manifestation" (Stuart Wilde)
3. The correct sequence is Be-Do-Have, not Have-Do-Be as some would think!

Examples:

- Reverse Be-Do-Have #1: "If only I had the money to go to college and get a degree, I could get a good job and make a good living!"
- Correct Be-Do-Have: "I am a college graduate, have a great job, and make a great living!"

- Reverse #2: "If I had a sponsor and patron, I could train for the Olympics and have a shot at a gold medal!"

- Correct: "I won a gold medal at the next Olympics!"

Do you see the difference?

"To be, do, and have or not to be, do, and have…that *is* the question." You must *be* in order to correctly *do* to create the desired *have*! Therefore, if your *havingness* is not ideal, then your *doingness* and ultimately *beingness* is not ideal, so correct them as is necessary.

4. Law of Attraction Exercise:

- Observe and write down any non-ideal circumstance or situation, big or small, in your life—business, relationships, money, career, health, etc.…

- Per the Law of Cause and Effect, your life situation (effect) corresponds directly to what you are BEING (cause), so assume and acknowledge that you are BEING that non-ideal circumstance, whether you believe this or not. This is called your responsibility level. If you can't or won't take responsibility, then you can never change anything!

- Compare your ideal Be-Do-Have with your current Be-Do-Have.

- Now BE the ideal circumstance—the opposite of the non-ideal situation. Think and feel what it would be like if you were being the ideal circumstance. Who would you be, what would you be doing, and what would you be having? Use your God-given gift of imagination and get incredibly detailed. To BE or not to BE, that *is* always the question!

- Do this daily and especially in the hypnagogic state before sleep when your conscious mind is relatively inactive. You want your subconscious mind—your personal interface to the *Invisible Architect* (the Infinite)— to really understand your desire so it can get busy (Law of Attraction).[33]

---

[33] Note: There's nothing blasphemous about demanding that the Infinite work for you! Remember, if the Infinite objected in the least to such a procedure, the thing could never happen. The Infinite is quite able to take care of itself.

- Advance Gratitude: Give thanks *in the present* as if your wish has already been achieved.

The purpose of this exercise is to correct your non ideal Be-Do-Have sequence because if your current life circumstance is unwanted, the cause that created that unwanted situation (effect) must be readjusted. Although you desired a tomato, you apparently planted some other type of seed, or the seed was damaged—you get the point? You must replant the correct seed (desire) into your subconscious garden and activate the *Invisible Architect* to attract the necessary people, places, and situations to allow that seed (desire) to grow into the intended desire—Law of Growth. Have patience because the way in which the Architect works its magic is unimaginable and may take time given the magnitude and clarity of your desire and the events that need to be orchestrated to fulfill it! (Revisit my stories in Cognition 2)

The Law of Attraction is simply…

Be + Do = Have

Correct Mindset + Correct Mechanics = Desired Reality

This is instantaneous in your mental universe but not so in the manifest universe, which has to obey the Law of Growth due to its denser frequencies and physics.

Q&A Cognition 10

1. Q: Who is the chief architect of your life?
    A: You are! You are responsible for creating your life blueprint and for supervising its construction until completion.

2. Q: What construction firm do you have at your disposal to carry out the completion of your life blueprint?
    A: The *Invisible Architect*, who is accessed through your subconscious mind through the correct spiritual mechanics.

3. Q: How can you discover your life's purpose if you're confused?
    A: Ask yourself what drives you, what are your natural talents and/or skills, what would you do if money was not an issue. Do you have any causes, charities, or people you'd like to help? Go into the silence, ask the *Invisible Architect*, and listen, listen, listen!

4. Q: If you've been trying to manifest your desires forever, but nothing is working, why is that?
    A: There are two reasons this could be so:
    - Ignorance of the spiritual mechanics involved.
    - Incorrect and inconsistent application of the fundamentals.

5. Q: What is the definition of spiritual mechanics?
    A: The relationship between the Universal Consciousness and its creations and the interactions thereof.

6. Q: What is the Be-Do-Have sequence?
   A: What you Are determines what you Do and what you will ultimately Have (Achieve).

7. Exercise: Review and study all the definitions in this Cognition.

8. Q: How does your subconscious mind work?
   A: Your subconscious mind is an unquestioning servant that creates your outer conscious world, consistent with your emotionalized thoughts and predominant beliefs.

9. Q: What is the Law of Correspondence?
   A: For you to change any unwanted effect (condition in the outer world), you must change its cause (condition in the inner world).

10. Q: What does it mean that you manifest what you are conscious of?
    A: If you are conscious (aware) of lack, limitation, sickness, stress, struggle, etc., that's what you will eventually manifest; if you are conscious (aware) of success, abundance, affluence, harmony, health, love, etc., that's what you will eventually manifest.

11. Q: What is the Law of Thought Substitution?
    A: In the physical realm, no two objects can occupy the same place at the same time; it's the same in the mental realm. Therefore, whenever you are challenged with an unwanted negative thought, a solution is to immediately replace that negative thought with a positive thought.

12. Q: What are the three states of mind when awake?
    A: Your mind is either in negative thought reverse mode and going backward toward unhappiness; a positive thought drive mode and going forward toward

happiness; or a no thought neutral mode—a static state of just being and perceiving, with no thought activity.

13. Q: What is the sleep state?
A: A condition of body and mind such as that which typically recurs for several hours every night, in which the nervous system is relatively inactive, the eyes closed, the postural muscles relaxed, and consciousness practically suspended.

14. Q: Short of mastering entering in and out of the state of neutral—pure being—what is the next solution to apply to your waking mind to further achieving your desires?
A: Being in the state of positive thoughts (drive) and using the Law of Thought Substitution whenever you find yourself in a negative thought state (reverse).

15. Drill: Postulate or affirm "I just am" when you find yourself in reverse moving toward unhappiness and see what happens.

16. Q: What is the Law of Opposites?
A: To be conscious of success you must be aware of its opposite: failure. If you began experiencing pushback toward achieving your desire, smile! Your manifestation is in progress; keep pushing ahead!

17. Q: What is the Law of Success?
A: Service, especially service to others!

18. Q: What is the Law of Giving?
A: Whatever you desire to receive, give. If you want joy, give joy; if you want money, give money!

19. Q: What is the Law of Attraction exercise?
A: Write down any undesirable circumstance you are

experiencing in your life. Now Be: imagine the opposite ideal circumstances. Do this daily especially before retiring. Eventually the *Invisible Architect* through your subconscious will come to your rescue proportionately to your belief and feeling and began manifesting your Have—your ideal circumstance.

Next Cognition…

Cognition 11
Guarding Your Mind

"Watch your thoughts; they become words. Watch your words; they become actions. Watch your actions; they become habits. Watch your habits; they become your character. Watch your character; they become your destiny."

—Buddha

"Behind every effect there is a cause, and if we follow the trail to its starting point, we shall find the creative principle out of which it grew. Proofs of this are now so complete that this truth is generally accepted."

—Charles Haanel

"What you think you Become. Your thoughts create you. What you DO you ARE. Your actions define you."

—Gordana Biernat

Spiritual Algebra: (Read at your own risk, especially if you failed algebra!)

Let's create a formula for manifestation. Suppose we…

Let (b) equal BE—the assumption of the beingness of your desire, the initial cause.

Let (d) equal DO—your imagination of the desire achieved (feeling) along with any supporting actions.

Let (h) equal HAVE—the desire achieved, the effect.

Then the simple formula would be…

b + d = h

Now what could make this formula fail or not be effective?

If (b) is the beingness, the cause, the thought or desire, then anything pushing back against (b) would be counterproductive or negative to that BE (thought, desire, cause, etc.) and so could be called a negative beingness, counter-thought, or counter-desire that can alter and alloy the original cause to the point where one unknowingly is operating on a false or altered cause. So, when the wrong effect (Have) occurs in the manifest universe (h̶), you think the Law of Cause and Effect is not working! That's false! It is working! It always works! It's just working with the altered or incorrect cause or beingness because you have allowed it to get corrupted due to ignorance. (For example, you desired a tomato plant but unknowingly planted something else like crabgrass, or maybe your tomato seed was damaged.)[34] This is the reason why so many fail with the Law of Attraction—allowing toxic counter-thoughts corrupt their desire. Additionally, it may be working perfectly but in ways you don't quite understand yet…so have patience! The *Invisible Architect* is a genius at reorganizing the Quantum Intelligent Field into your desire, but it takes time in this dimension of dense low frequencies!

ANY CAUSE YIELDS THE CORRESPONDING EFFECT, ALWAYS!

CORRECT CAUSE YIELDS THE DESIRED EFFECT, ALWAYS!

---

[34] It could also be possible that you knowingly wanted to fail for various reasons and so planted the wrong or bad seed! Why you would do this is beyond the scope of this manuscript.

INCORRECT CAUSE EQUALS UNDESIRED EFFECT, ALWAYS!

THE LAW OF ATTRACTION IS ALWAYS WORKING, ALWAYS!

So, if (c) = the counter-thought(s) that alter the original cause proportionate to their strength, the formula now is altered:

b - c + d = < h to h̶

(b) original cause minus (c) counter-thought + a weak or altered (d) equals less than or no desire achieved. (<h to h̶)

The new cause is not the original because the counter-thought, or thoughts, have altered it and so produce a different usually unwanted outer-world effect!

< h to h̶ means less than the original desire or no desire achieved contingent to how corrupted the original desire (b) became!

(b) - (c) where (c) is any counter-thought to (b) your original desire = (h) partially not achieved to the degree that (c) is bigger, equal to, or less than the original (b) desire or thought.

Note: If your original cause is strong and the counter-effort (pushback) is small or weak, then you might still get close to the original desire, which explains the original desire being slightly modified. Let's make this clearer with a real-life example:

Say your stated achieved desire is "I am a successful pro golfer earning over a million per year!"

You clearly and repetitively plant this seed (Be) into your subconscious personal garden, inviting the *Invisible Architect* (Do) to begin using its powers to work its magic and attract everything you will need to be proactive and support and amplify its work toward that stated reality.[35]

Now, let's say you allow negative thoughts and/or doubts to enter your garden and mess with your pro golfer seed. If you don't handle this and do it quickly, your seed will be slowed, damaged, or destroyed ("the birds might eat it," as success author Jim Rohn stated) and the desire will proportionately be attenuated. Why? Because you will incorrectly evaluate that you have failed to the degree that you allowed the counter-thoughts, emotions, and efforts into your mental space and prevent manifestation. You will assume the Law of Attraction isn't working, when in fact it's working perfectly and manifesting your predominant desire, which we now know you have allowed to be altered with either internal or external counter-thoughts.

But you're thinking, "Wait a minute! The Invisible Architect is all-knowing and all-powerful, so that shouldn't be a problem, as my original desire was clear and pure!" I thought that, too, but the key word here is "was"! Your original desire indeed might have been perfectly clear, but it isn't now due to your allowing it to be alloyed. Apparently, the way this paradigm was created, which is above my pay grade, the *Invisible Architect* must immediately act on our *current* predominant thoughts and beliefs, whether they're clear and focused, unclear and uncertain, constantly changing, confusing, opposite, etc. (Remember the taxicab example?)

Is there a quick fix? Yes, by applying a little *spiritual science* to the formula as soon as you become aware of any pushback (counter-thinking) to your original desire.

Spiritual Science

In the Physical Universe, no two objects (pieces of solid matter—even though we know that matter is not solid and just condensed energy—can occupy the same space at the same time. Example: two cars

---

[35]Note: Sitting around doing nothing, thinking you're not part of the equation, is pure irresponsibility and laziness. That is one of the major misapplications people make when applying the Law of Attraction.

colliding, an asteroid hitting a planet, a human being running into a brick wall). It also explains why we don't fall through the ground when we're walking. Now, I know there is complicated physics regarding this phenomenon—for example, the Pauli Exclusion Principle in Quantum Particles discusses particle repulsion—but we don't need to go that deep for this spiritual exercise. When it comes to human beings and thoughts, it appears that no two thoughts can actively be thought of simultaneously—in sequence, yes, but not simultaneously. In other words, if you are worrying about money, you can't at the same time be entertaining any other thought, positive or negative. You can move from one thought to another at thought speed, but you can't "think" about more than one thought at a time—at least I can't![36]

The quick fix is a) become an expert at detecting these desire thieves (counter-thoughts) as soon as they happen, and b) immediately use the Law of Thought Substitution to keep your original desire intact![37]

Background

Unless you are at an advanced spiritual state and can just Be in the now and perceive without thinking, which as discussed earlier is possible with disciplined practice but not very practical is this action-dimension, your mind is always thinking thoughts and constantly moving from one to another, positive or negative. It's almost impossible to let go of a thought without replacing it with another thought. But all is not lost, as we can use this phenomenon—replacing thoughts—to our advantage. It's difficult and takes practice but is an important skill to learn and apply.

---

[36]And it is a good thing because The National Science Foundation published an article in 2005 showing the average mind thinks between 12,000 and 60,000 thoughts a day. That's an average of 500 to 2,500 thoughts per hour. Of those, 80% are negative and 95% are the same repetitive thoughts as the day before! That's incredible! Imagine if we could think multiple thoughts simultaneously. It would probably cause instant insanity!

[37] Your original desire must not only be clear and focused but remain that way during the entire manifestation process!

Application

We just discussed that no two objects can occupy the same location at the same time in the Physical Universe, right? Well, this phenomenon of matter can also be applied to the thought universe and assist you in manifesting your desires.

Remember the formula $b - c + d = \, < h$ to $\hbar$ where (c) is counter-thinking? If we can apply the Law of Thought Substitution as soon as any counter-thought (c) comes into your mind and immediately replace it with a better thought or the correct original thought for the situation, the Law of Attraction, which is always at work, will work more in your favor and manifest your desire. Why? Because your *subjective* desire will eventually *objectify or manifest* in the reality universe if clear, focused, sustained and made with no distractive counter-thinking. This is the Law of Correspondence or Cause = Effect.[38]

Example: You have the goal redefined that you are the top salesman at your company, earning a six-figure per year income. You've stated it clearly and planted it into your subconscious multiple times a day and at night during the hypnagogic state. You're doing everything correctly. You're imagining the desire fulfilled, you're visualizing and feeling what your life would be like when achieved, you're getting excited, you're supporting it with your actions etc., but your mind is pushing back (Law of Opposites) with thoughts such as...

---

[38]When I hear someone complain that the Law of Attraction is not working, my answer is, "Hell it's not!" It's working perfectly as it always does! It's just not working in your favor due to your ignorance of the spiritual mechanics involved. This is important to understand. It is a Spiritual Law and always has the same observed cause and effect relationship. If your desire (cause) is not clear—has doubt and uncertainty in it—then the effect will be altered accordingly. If you don't understand this, you will incorrectly conclude the Law of Attraction doesn't work!

"I'll never be the top salesman—who am I kidding?"
"This Law of Attraction stuff is BS!"
"My dad worked hard and died poor; so will I!"
"I'm behind on my mortgage; this top salesman desire isn't working!"

The moment these doubts and uncertainties—counter-thoughts—enter your mental universe, whether from within or without, substitute the correct desire, such as:

"I am the top salesman at my company, earning six figures a year!"
"The Law of Attraction works—I know it does!"
"I work hard and am very successful!"
"I have plenty of money to handle all my needs and more!"

Disagree with your senses. They're just giving you feedback about the *current* reality; we're in the process of changing that undesired reality.

You can never change any reality if you continue to agree with it!

This is what is meant about guarding your desires. It doesn't matter if it's your huge overall life career goal or a simple "I feel great today" desire; the thought substitution works every time and works immediately once you acquire the skillset to use it.

By the way, if you are having a bad day and are down in the dumps, try affirming repeatedly the following affirmations and see what happens.

"I'm having a great day!"
"I feel great!"
"I am happy!"

Kick Out the Mental Thieves!

You affirm: "I'm wealthy!" Your friend says: "Give me a break! You believe in that Law of Attraction nonsense! We both know you're poor!" Eventually, you start agreeing with him; you've let a *dream thief* into your mind's home. When this happens, your original desire (cause) is altered proportionate to how much you agree with these mental thieves and their toxic comments. And it makes no difference if mental thieves come from *your* inner world or the outer world.

You have a desire to be a schoolteacher, so you affirm, "I am a successful schoolteacher!" You have the talent, you love children, and you can feel the love and success! A special documentary comes on TV about not only how teachers are underpaid but also how horrible and dangerous the education system is, etc. You become uncertain about your career choice. You should have disagreed with that reality immediately and restated your Be (desire) clearly and with excited *feelings*, but instead you unlocked your door and let in the dream thief, and the dwindling spiral of that desire began! And since most do not know the spiritual mechanics we're discussing, this all happens below your radar unconsciously.

Any External Source Agreed With Can Steal Your Desires!

Guard Your Mind Castle!

Q&A Cognition 11

1. Q: What is the formula for manifestation? Explain this
    formula in your own words.
    A: Be +Do = Have, which could be stated as b + d = h

2. Q: If the original desire (Be) is corrupted, is altered by
    some negative or counter-thought, emotion, or belief,
    then to that degree, the original desire is thwarted. How
    would that change the formula?
    A: $b - c + d = < h$ to h, which translates to your original
    desire being negatively altered to the point that your
    manifestation is less than or not at all achieved. ($<h$ to h)

3. Q: How is the thought substitution applied to the
    manifestation formula?

    A: As soon as any negative counter-thought (pushback)
    enters your mind castle, whether from within or without,
    immediately replace it with a better thought or the
    correct thought for the situation. Now the Law of
    Attraction has a chance to work in your favor and
    manifest *your* desire.

4. Q: What is meant by guarding your desires?
    A: Don't let "mental thieves"—thoughts or beliefs
    counter to your desires—steal your dreams! Whether
    they come from within or without, kick out these mental
    thieves immediately using thought substitution.

Next Cognition…

Cognition 12
Spiritual Marksmanship

"Where your mind goes, energy flows."

—*Ernest Holmes*

"Everything that exists has being, has God-essence, has some degree of consciousness. Consciousness is the light emanating from the eternal Source. Being, consciousness and life are synonymous.

—*Eckhart Tolle*

"We need only in cold blood ACT as if the thing in question were real, and keep ACTING as if it were real, and it will infallibly end by growing into such a connection with our life that it will become real."

—*William James*

Since we already have the *Invisible Architect* within us or assigned to us—however you want to think of it—we don't need to look for or acquire it. We just need to be conscious of it. Our consciousness becomes conscious of itself—life attaining self-consciousness or the awareness of its awareness. But understanding this self- awareness is important to be able to use it—or it will use you!

Spiritual Marksmanship

So, what is the best way to employ this energy in our daily lives, to hit the target each time, so it becomes our new modus operandi?

It takes consistent practice to change one's modus operandi. To operate the Be-Do-Have sequence correctly, you must always approach every desire, large or small, from Be (cause). You must put your energy, your attention, on the desire, and not on the undesirable circumstance you're trying to change. You must be what you wish or will to be.

As the quote below says:

"Where your mind goes, energy flows." —Ernest Holmes (*The Science of Mind*)

Therefore, your energy must be put predominantly on the desire (Be), and the imagination (visualization) of the desire achieved and supporting actions (Do) from you, not on the unwanted situation in the form of stress, worry, "I have to solve this or else," etc.

Remember, it's the Law of Cause and Effect, not the Law of Effect and then Cause! It's better to simply affirm the non-optimum circumstance as handled by stating the wish as fulfilled.

Example: "Oh, my God, if I don't get my mortgage up to date, the bank will foreclose my house!"

That may be true, but stating that and worrying about it just validates what *you* are causing to be imminent. You're making it your predominant thought; not a good idea! This modus operandi continues its creation in the Quantum Intelligent Field where all energy and frequencies exist awaiting to be reorganized by the observer.

Affirming "I have plenty of money to get my mortgage up to date" even though reality says otherwise is how to correctly use the spiritual mechanics of BE + DO = HAVE to change your reality. Also, operating this way, if done correctly and consistently, attracts other positive energy, frequencies, and ideas to solve the situation and at the same time eradicates stress and worry—a win-win!

A stressed mind cannot see solutions!

When the mind is engaged in stress, worry, fear—negative toxic emotions—it's impossible to be happy, excited, enthusiastic, and inspired, as no two thoughts and/or emotions happen simultaneously. And you cannot retrieve those moments back in your life. And not only does chronic stress damage tissues in the body through the continual exposure to harmful stress hormones, it also interferes with sleep and makes you no fun to be around—pretty much a dwindling spiral.

Recent research reveals we spend on average one hour and fifty minutes a day stressing, amounting to twelve hours and fifty-three minutes a week—or four years and eleven months across the average adult lifetime of sixty-four years. Personally, I think it's much higher than that! And guess what? Eighty-five percent of the things people worry about never happen!

There's a big difference between being proactive about a situation and finding a solution and unnecessary, destructive worry and stress. The latter does nothing to solve the problem and, if anything, makes it worse. Besides that, lower-frequency emotions do not contribute to bright ideas and solutions, which is why focusing your energy on the *problem solved*, rather than the problem unsolved, is the way to operate. This cannot be over-emphasized!

Now some say this positive type of thinking is dangerous, as it promotes a no-responsibility, do-nothing approach to life. Not true! They're just uniformed and don't know the spiritual mechanics here. The affirmation must be clear and positive to change one's mindset to BE instead of NOT BE. Positive thinking, as discussed earlier, doesn't mean you don't act (DO) to support your goal redefined. Yes, that would be irresponsible. On the contrary, the positive statement will inspire more constructive thoughts and consequent productive actions versus reactive thoughts and unproductive actions or apathy and zero actions!

Like thoughts and beliefs attract more of the same!

Also, if you're worrying about it, the *Invisible Architect* does not actively begin attracting what you need to achieve your desire. It just acknowledges your worry (this is a personification, of course, as I do not know the exact mechanism here). If anything, the Architect thinks you *desire* more worry, which you will undoubtedly attract and surely don't need.

Now don't just believe me. As an experiment, try worrying and stressing about a non-optimum circumstance in your life and observe how your worry attracts more and more worry and stress. If not stopped, it will just continue the negative situation, make it worse, and can even lead into depression. In other words, some unknowingly cause their own depression! And as mentioned previously, most of the time these events never happen anyway. It's just wasted energy!

Simply write down every time you become aware of your negative thoughts and how much time you wrestle with them.

The interesting thing about this exercise is that by just taking inventory, you will become more aware of them and naturally reduce these unproductive negative mental meanderings drastically. For the ones you have difficulty with, simply substitute positive thoughts in their place repetitively until these mental thieves are chased away!

Self-Awareness Exercise: It is especially important to be fully aware of the *Invisible Architect's* existence and your relationship with it. Otherwise, it's impossible to interact with and use this power constructively and efficiently.

Since Be is the first step of existence, let alone manifestation, go into that special state we call the Silence and know (become conscious or aware) that you exist—ARE (Be).

To manifest anything, the next step is to become conscious that YOU ARE (x) where (x) is anything you desire to manifest.

I AM THAT I AM: MEANS I AM (x), I AM[39] where (x) is your desire, your Be.

Example: "I AM affluent." "I Am" means I am affluent, I really am! (Proclamation!)

Or "I am what I decide to become!"

"I am what I will to be!"

You are stating your desire as already having been achieved and then proclaiming it to the Quantum Energy Field (the *Invisible Architect*)—God, if you so choose that reference—so it clearly knows your desire and begins the Do activity of the Be-Do-Have formula—the Law of Attraction. Since you and the *Invisible Architect* are a team, trust me; you will become aware of what you need to be doing to support and amplify the *Invisible Architect's* behind-the-scenes work.

Drill: Go into the Silence and focus on Being that which you desire. The Do actions or activities will naturally follow with the help of the *Invisible Architect*. Finish off the exercise with advance gratitude!

And remember, patience is a virtue because, as we previously discussed, the dense frequencies and physics of the Physical Universe take considerable time and effort to reorganize (the Law of Growth), compared to the thought universe, which is instantaneous (the speed of thought!).

---

[39] "I am that I am"—These are the words written in the spiritual literature of the Torah, also called the Pentateuch—the first five books of the Old Testament, in which God tells Moses that "this is my name forever, a name by which I shall be known for all future generations"— "I am That I am." —Dr. Wayne Dyer, mediation, https://www.youtube.com/watch?v=A96OI4b8sFY

Achieving Any Desire

For any desire you wish to achieve or a current non-optimum situation you would like to solve, simply apply the following Be-Do-Have formula:

Be: State the desire or situation to change as already fulfilled!
Do: Imagine the desire already achieved in your life in detail. How would your life in every aspect be changed for the better? Your actions will support and amplify as is necessary!
Have: Give advance gratitude to the Architect for your desire achieved.

Example #1 Situation: You're sick!

Be-Do-Have Solution:

Be: "I am healthy." (Be in the present in your personal thought universe what you wish to be!)
Do: Imagine multiple times daily, especially before sleep, that you are getting a good night's sleep every night. You are totally healthy and back to your old self, back to work, with no more symptoms or attention to your body or any other details—overall indicative of how you would be acting if you were totally healthy!
Have: Give advance gratitude to the Universal Energy (*Invisible Architect*) multiple times every day, especially at night as you fall asleep, for your healthy body and renewed strength, etc. Give thanks in as many ways as you can think of and really mean it!

Sidebar: Ignore reality and any pushback from your mind saying it isn't so! Just use the Law of Substitution if any negative counter-thoughts to your stated desire enter your mind whether from within or from any source without. Just restate "I am healthy" to replace any counter-thoughts as many times as necessary and remember why you're doing this—no two thoughts can be active at the same time![40]

---

[40]Important: These exercises are mental spiritual exercises to assist your recovery. If you are sick, please make sure you seek professional medical care.

Example #2 Situation: You and your girlfriend are angry with each other and separated!

Be-Do-Have Solution:

Be: "My girlfriend and I are back together and in great communication!"
Do: Imagine multiple times every day that you and your girlfriend have forgiven each other, are back together again, are going for coffee like you used to do, talking and having a good time, etc. Add as much detail as possible.
Have: Give advance gratitude multiple times every day, especially at night as you fall asleep, for you and your girlfriend being back together and whole again! Give thanks in as many ways as you can think of.

Remember: Ignore reality (your outer world) and any pushback from your mind (inner world) saying it isn't so! Just use the Law of Substitution if any negative counter-thoughts enter your mental universe, whether from within or from without. If they do and they will, just restate your goal redefined: "My girlfriend and I are back together and in great communication," or whatever positive wording works for you. Do this as many times as is necessary to keep your energy focused on your inner world!

Example #3 Situation: Chronic lack of money!

Be-Do-Have Solution:

Be: "Money is circulating freely in my life; I always have a surplus!"
Do: Imagine multiple times every day that your bank account has plenty of money for your needs! See yourself paying all your bills on time, increasing your savings account, buying new clothes, purchasing plenty of groceries with no stress because you now have plenty of money. Add as much detail as possible.
Have: Give gratitude multiple times every day, especially at night as you fall asleep, to the *Invisible Architect* or Universal Consciousness, God,

Jesus—whatever name works for you for now having a surplus of money and affluence! Give thanks in as many ways as you can think of and really mean it.

Important: Ignore the fact that you still have a scarcity of money. The way this works is you must convince your subconscious—the *Invisible Architect*—that you are now wealthy! It doesn't matter whether it's true or not—how cool is that? Just use the Law of Substitution if any negative thoughts enter your mental universe whether from within or from without. Just restate any counter-thoughts with "I have plenty of money for every demand I run into," etc.—or whatever positive wording works for you, as many times as necessary. Have patience as the *Invisible Architect* works its magic in ways you cannot imagine!

Example #4 Situation: Stage fright going out during your auditions!

Be-Do-Have Solution:

Be: "I am totally prepared for this audition and feel 100 percent confident that I have done my best!" Notice I did not say "I will do my best"; I said that "I *have done* my best"—goal redefined!

Do: Imagine multiple times every day especially before falling asleep that you did a great performance and got the part. See yourself showing up to the set, meeting with the director for blocking, going over your lines, going to makeup and wardrobe, and even seeing your stage name on the dressing room door. See your friends and family congratulating you and, hey, if it's a major part in a great movie, nothing wrong with seeing yourself getting nominated for an Oscar and even winning, right? Whatever speaks to you! Add as much detail as possible—it's your script!

Have: Give thanks and appreciation multiple times every day, especially at night as you fall asleep, to the *Invisible Architect* or Quantum Energy Field, Cosmic Consciousness—whatever name works for you—for having gotten the acting role that opened the door to your acting career, etc. Give thanks in as many ways as you can think!

Important: Ignore reality and any pushback from your mind saying it isn't so! Just use the Law of Substitution if any negative counter-thoughts to your desire enter your mental universe whether from within or from any source without. Just say, "I am totally prepared and confident for this and any audition"—whatever positive wording works for you—as many times necessary to replace any counter-thoughts. By now I'm sure you got the idea!

The *Invisible Architect* can also be contacted to receive information. After all, the Intelligent Energy Field is omni or all-everything! It is all-powerful, all-knowing, all-present, all-loving, all-patient, all-forgiving, all-infinite, all-perfect, etc. So, whenever you need an answer to any situation—any situation at all—do the following:

Go into the silence with nobody around and no distractions. I suggest even wearing a blackout mask or being in a room that can be prepped to be totally dark.[41]

The reason for this is that the *Invisible Architect* communicates from a high, subtle frequency and so to tune in, you need to be 100 percent attentive to any answers you receive. From my experience, these answers are sometimes as clear as a person standing next to you talking or simple intuitive hunches and anything in between.

Tip: Sometimes the answers come in the form of dreams. I have a pen and pencil near my bed and have gotten into a habit that anytime I wake up, I immediately scan my mind to see if I had any dreams that might have had some information in answer to my question.

You can, of course, ask the *Invisible Architect* about anything. (See **Cognition 2** for some of my personal questions and answers.)

---

[41]"Learn to keep the door shut, keep out of your mind and out of your world every element that seeks admittance with no definite helpful end in view."—George Matthew Adams

Example: You're trying to figure out whether to quit your job now, as it's very suppressive and not earning you enough income, but you have no other job to take its place. Well...ask the Architect. "Should I quit and see what happens? Put my resume on websites? What should I do? Please advise."

You might get an answer like "Call cousin Ronnie," which may confuse you. But don't question the advice; just trust the Architect and just do it! You might call Cousin Ronnie and say, "Hey Ronnie, You okay? I was thinking of you the other day." The next thing you know, you begin catching up and you find out he just lost his digital marketer, leaving an open job that matches part of your skill set, and bingo! Now this was a fictional example but a good representation of the things that can and will happen once you develop an awareness of the Architect and learn how to ask and listen.

Or you might get an answer like "Hang in there; your boss is going to get fired"!

If you recall in **Cognition 2**, I asked the *Invisible Architect* the following:

"Okay, I'm out West in Los Angeles, don't know anybody, and I'm broke as hell. Now what?"

The answer that came in the form of an idea was "Hang out at all the jazz clubs and major music stores to network."

Lo and behold, the keyboardist of a new band A Taste of Honey heard me playing at the Guitar Center in Los Angeles where I used to go to network per my inner voice advice. He took my contact info, and three months later, his band's first record on Capitol Records got released and became a big hit selling millions and I became their musical director. Who would have figured? Money problem solved, among other things, as this gig opened many musical doors!

Once you get the hang of this, you'll enjoy having your own all-knowing guru giving you advice on anything you ask.

Examples:

"Should I move to Los Angeles?"

"How am I going to afford my daughter's college?"

"Should I invest in this stock I was referred to?"

"My son is being bullied in school; how should I handle this?"

"I'm looking for a soulmate. Please help."

"These migraines are ruining my life! What should I do?"

Sidebar: Some of these questions could be turned into the Be-Do-Have exercise as well (see above).

Your inner world will help create your outer world if you understand the spiritual mechanics of manifestation. The real work consists in your convincing yourself of the truth of this information through observation and experience rather than theory or pure logic or because someone said so. When you have succeeded in doing this and you have no doubts and reservations, you will have no difficulty in achieving your desires. This what is meant by the phrase *designing your life from within!*

The truth will surely then set you free!

Q&A Cognition 12

1. Q: How do I acquire my own *Invisible Architect* for use?
   A: You already have the *Invisible Architect* within you!

2. Q: What then is the best way to employ the *Invisible Architect* in my daily life?
   A: You must BE what you WISH or WILL to be. Where your mind goes, energy flows.

3. Q: What is the procedure?
   A: Put your thoughts predominantly on the desire and use your imagination (visualization) of the desire achieved, not on the unwanted situation. It's a cause that manifests the effect, not the effect that manifests the cause.

4. Q: Why is a stressed mind not ideal?
   A: A stressed mind cannot see solutions. It is engaged in worry, fear, etc.—negative emotions that make it difficult to clearly communicate your desires to the *Invisible Architect*. Chronic stress also damages your body through continual exposure to harmful stress hormones, not to mention how it interferes with sleep.[42]

5. Do the Negative Mental Inventory Exercise outlined in this Cognition.

6. Q: What is the procedure for contacting the *Invisible Architect* to receive advice and counsel?
   A: Go into the Silence with no distractions. Then be 100 percent totally attentive to answers you may receive, but remember the

---

[42]A study published in PNAS found that chronic stress caused a failure to down-regulate the body's inflammatory response, causing an increase in inflammation without the ability to decrease it again. This increase in plasma cortisol concentration then caused an increased risk of disease exposure.

Invisible Architect communicates from a high God-Frequency. Pay attention!

Next Cognition…

Cognition 13
How to Create Miracles![43]

"For every minute you remain angry, you give up sixty seconds of peace of mind."

—Ralph Waldo Emerson

"Forgiveness isn't approving what happened. It's choosing to rise above it."

—Robin Sharma

"Forgiveness is the fragrance that the violet sheds on the heel that has crushed it."

—Mark Twain

"Gratitude is the healthiest of all human emotions. The more you express gratitude for what you have, the more likely you will have even more to express gratitude for."

—Zig Ziglar

"There are only two ways to live your life. One is as though nothing is a miracle. The other is as though everything is a miracle."

—Albert Einstein

"Some people grumble that roses have thorns; I am grateful that thorns have roses."

—Alphonse Karr

---

[43] These quotes are all very enlightening and so important to understand, as they relate to creating miracles in your life!

141

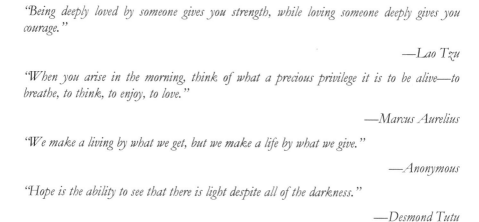

"Being deeply loved by someone gives you strength, while loving someone deeply gives you courage."

—*Lao Tzu*

"When you arise in the morning, think of what a precious privilege it is to be alive—to breathe, to think, to enjoy, to love."

—*Marcus Aurelius*

"We make a living by what we get, but we make a life by what we give."

—*Anonymous*

"Hope is the ability to see that there is light despite all of the darkness."

—*Desmond Tutu*

"Faith goes up the stairs that love has built and looks out the windows which hope has opened."

—*Charles Haddon Spurgeon*

The power of love, giving, forgiveness, gratitude, and hope can be truly life-changing and miraculous if truly understood and applied in your life!

Although the many quotes above speak for themselves, I'd like to add some additional insight from my experience about why and how these wonderful feelings can help create miracles in your life, especially when they are causative versus reactive to an event or situation.

We have already established that our inner world of thoughts and beliefs contribute greatly to our outer reality circumstances and more so than you probably think. So, logically, if our inner world is predominantly loving, giving, forgiving, and full of gratitude and hope, it follows that it will be much easier to apply the spiritual mechanics of the Law of Cause and Effect or the Be-Do-Have formula. After all, these are Godly traits, yes? The closer we are to the God-Frequencies, the easier it will be to employ the *Invisible Architect* to design our lives!

Have you ever tried to work with somebody who you couldn't relate to or who you couldn't communicate with?

If the *Invisible Architect*, the Intelligent Energy Field that permeates everything, is the cause of everything, is ALL, then it is logical that the closer our union is with this intelligent energy, the more effective we become in manifesting our desires. And what if every constructive desire we have is actually the *Invisible Architect's* urge to know itself through us, one of its unique creations? Well, if this is the case, and I believe it is, it wouldn't be a good idea to ignore these attributes—love, giving, forgiveness, gratitude, and hope—let alone not master and use them in your daily life, right?

So, if God is all-loving, all-giving, all-forgiving, all-grateful, and all-hopeful and everything, including life, are its creations, then this intelligent energy is within us. It follows, then, that we have the same attributes, and so by practicing these attributes in our daily lives, we evolve closer to our true spiritual roots. D

Miracle: 1. A surprising and welcome event that is not explicable by natural or scientific laws and is therefore considered to be the work of a Divine agency; 2. A highly improbable or extraordinary event, development, or accomplishment that brings very welcome consequences.

If you recall from **Cognition 2**, "Awareness of the Architect," my list of interactions with the *Invisible Architect* contains some miraculous events, events I cannot explain naturally. Employing these feelings in our daily lives opens the communication line and interaction with the *Invisible Architect* where everything exists and anything is possible!

Let's look at each one of these jewels from a practical viewpoint:

To Forgive: 1.to grant pardon for or remission of (an offense, debt, etc.); 2. To absolve; 3. To cease to feel resentment against.

The bottom line is that unresolved conflicts take up way too much mental space—thought energy—in your mind. Withholding forgiveness is a drain on our energy reserves that could be better used to serve others and enrich your own life. Every unresolved conflict also includes negative toxic emotions (bitterness, anger, resentment, revenge, etc.), which weigh heavily on your mind and body. Releasing these toxic emotions is very freeing, therapeutic, and uplifting and contributes greatly to your personal growth. Holding on to these toxic emotions therefore usurps more and more of your mental energy, not only making you less able to Be-Do-Have but also further creating your own mental prison. True forgiveness, therefore, frees up space in your mind, allowing you to escape this self-created prison.

To clear up any confusion on this process, forgiving someone doesn't mean you are pardoning or excusing the other person's actions. It doesn't even necessarily mean you need to tell the person that they are forgiven. Forgiving is mainly for your mindset and spiritual development so you can be free of the situation. If you wish to tell the person you are forgiving them, then good for you! It will help free them, too, because trust me: If they wronged you, they probably have trapped negative energy in their space, too. And in some cases, they may not even know they have wronged you, and so you may be repairing a relationship. It is your gift to them; hence, "for giving!" But if not, don't feel guilty; the act of forgiving is mainly for your growth.

And by the way, forgiving doesn't mean you aren't allowed to still have feelings about the situation, or that you must like the person, or that everything is okay, or that you must include them in your life.

Without forgiveness, the world would even be worse off than it is, given the accumulative hatred. What the world needs is forgiveness and more honesty and love!

That said…let's not forget forgiving oneself first!

Giving: 1. to present voluntarily and without expecting compensation; bestow; 2. providing love or other emotional support; 3. caring.

Giving is a miracle in itself! It is the beginning of our transformation into higher beings. It is not only an economic exchange; it is an act of generosity. It does not subtract from the giver; it in fact multiplies for the giver and the world. If one's inner world consists of a feeling of abundance and sharing, then there is a natural urge to give, to share that abundance. Reversely, if you have a goal of inner abundance in any area—love, money, inspiration, peace, health, etc.—then practice giving the same, and you shall reap a thousand-fold!

I believe it was Buddha who said that:

"No true spiritual life is possible without a generous heart."

Err on the side of extravagant generosity and become God-like. Why? Because everything we have and accomplish comes from the *Invisible Architect's* love for us. And we probably would not be alive, nor could we accomplish much of anything, without the support, love, and generosity of all the people who have helped us become who we are now! Certainly, it is from experiencing this generosity from the Spirit—that from which we are—and the generosity of those in our life, that we should learn to give and receive love and be giving and generous to others.

Loving: A deep, intense feeling of affection and solicitude toward a person or thing, such as that arising from a sense of oneness.

This is a good definition, especially the part of oneness, but I think there's more.

The Bible says, "Love is patient, love is kind. It does not envy, it does not boast, it is not proud. It does not dishonor others, it is not self-seeking, it is not easily angered, it keeps no record of wrongs" (1 Corinthians 13:4-5).

This describes some behaviors of being loving, but isn't really a definition.

Let's take the phrase "a sense of oneness":

My understanding, based upon my experience, is that love is becoming one with something! There would be no distance or separation between the lover and the lovee! As an example, in a loving relationship, the feeling of love and oneness is wonderful; but if an unresolved problem enters the relationship, that wonderful feeling becomes lost, and there's a perception of distance or separation. Something's broken, in other words, which continues until the problem is resolved and the affinity restored!

Or how about being one with a musical instrument like the piano? Your love is so great that when you play, you ARE the piano and the piano IS you! You are ONE! You are congruent—in total harmony! Some call that "being in the zone." Many athletes describe that being and staying in the zone is the secret to top performance!

Is this the Be in the Be-Do-Have sequence? You BEING the piano, the music?

And if you are indeed ONE, then it follows that your performance (Do) would be effortless and inspirational, and you and your audience would delight in the result (Have)!

The Law of Cause and Effect are one. Cause is effect; effect is cause…They are each other; they are LOVE!

Remember…**Everything** consists of **Energy**.

If everything is energy, then everything is connected and not separate. If this is so, then we are essentially ONE (love) even though we are unique beings with different energy signatures.[44]

Love is attraction; hatred is repulsion!

Since everything is energy, including you and me, then everything is an expression of the affinity and cohesion of the particles that make up energy. Nonexistence, then, would be the opposite of the affinity and cohesion (love) of these particles (hate), as it would be the absence of their attraction and agreement. Some things therefore unite harmoniously in composition; some become discordant and so repelling of each other that they decompose, and nonexistence results. Everything

---

[44]"I am he as you are he as you are me and we are all together." "I Am The Walrus," Lennon & McCartney

is subject to this principle, and so the Be-Do-Have creative process in all its degrees of variation is an expression or outcome of love.

LOVE = EXISTENCE   NO LOVE = NONEXISTENCE

Gratitude: The word *gratitude* is derived from the Latin word *gratia*, which means grace, graciousness, or gratefulness (depending on the context). Gratitude is a thankful appreciation for what an individual receives, whether tangible or intangible. With gratitude, people acknowledge the goodness in their lives. In the process, people usually recognize that the source of that goodness lies at least partially outside themselves. As a result, gratitude also helps people connect to something larger than themselves as individuals—whether to other people, nature, or a higher power.

Gratitude can be expressed in multiple ways—toward the past as in being thankful for past blessings, toward the present as in being thankful for good blessings as they happen, and toward the future as in maintaining a hopeful and optimistic attitude and/or, as discussed earlier, a type of advance gratitude used in the Be-Do-Have sequence, which assists greatly in the manifestation process.

Gratitude is a way for people to appreciate what they have, instead of always reaching for something new in the hopes it will make them happier or thinking they can't feel satisfied in the present until every physical and material need is met. Gratitude helps people refocus on what they have instead of what they lack. And, although it may feel contrived at first, this mindset grows stronger with use and practice.

Also, a grateful mind is a happy one! Since we established that no two thoughts can be thought of simultaneously, the more often your mind is filled with gratefulness, the happier and more optimistic you are.

High-frequency qualities such as love, giving, forgiveness, gratefulness, and hope not only attract similar high frequencies from the Quantum Field but also amplify the achievement of your desires!

Besides enhancing the manifestation process, practicing gratitude improves relationships, physical and mental health, sleep, self-esteem, and empathy while also reducing the toxic emotions of selfishness, negativity, aggression, complaining, stress, and worry!

Gratitude is probably the most powerful prayer you can say. It's the most impactful habit and mindset you can develop if you want to experience your life and the world in a more positive light.

Gratitude is the best attitude!

Hope: In general, hope means to desire with expectation of obtainment or fulfillment; to expect with confidence. Hope is not wishful thinking. It's a viewpoint that despite life's challenges and misfortunes, all will work out! There is something else beyond this moment.

An applicable quote that always gives me strength is:

"This too shall pass."—Og Mandino, *The Greatest Salesman in the World*

This quote or datum can be applied to any undesirable situation: sickness, poverty, a job loss, an upcoming tax audit, heartache, or any life adversity.

You can do incredible things with hope! It changes your mindset from one of being a victim to one of being a survivor! If you have hope, you have a life; you can recover from almost anything. If hope was a pill, it would be the most powerful antidepressant ever, and if it could be patented, it would probably sell for a million dollars, given its demand and ability to create life-changing miracles!

"But it's hard to have hope in the midst of darkness," you say! Right you are, but you now have a secret weapon! It's called the Law of Thought Substitution. Remember how it works? Just substitute a positive thought when you find your mind predominantly overwhelmed with an undesirable thought. By doing this you are your own *spiritual pharmacist* and creating your own organic antidepressant pill...and for free! How amazing is that?

Application: You're deeply depressed about the loss of your dog, so by all means grieve! It's healthy to express your love in this case in the form of grief. But when you want to get back in the game, go to your personal pharmacy and purchase a positive thought pill like "My dog was my best friend—I love him," pop it into your mental universe, and digest! Hope pills can be taken on an empty stomach or with food but are best taken immediately at the first sign of depression!

Another example: You are overwhelmed with depression and/or unhappiness. Nothing is going right in your eyes. Substitute "I am happy, life is fantastic!" Yes, your mind will give you some pushback thoughts like "that's not true," "you're nuts," "you're in denial, dummy," etc. Ignore and continue your positive affirmation thought because, remember, like thoughts attract like thoughts, and soon your mind will be filled with better thoughts—I swear!

Analogy: If you had an unbearable itch on your back, wouldn't you just scratch it? Of course! Same with an unbearable thought. Why put up with that thought? Just scratch it, meaning replace it with a better thought, and after a while you will become master of your thoughts, which is a miracle unto itself given how destructive unwanted thoughts can be to your life.

Remember...the seeds of hope are more fertile than the seeds of doubt, and the qualities of love, giving, forgiveness, and gratitude can be catalysts for creating miracles in your life, but only if you practice them diligently.

The *Invisible Architect* responds to the vibrations you are putting out there; it is neutral. Like vibrations attract like vibrations—it's that simple. If you're sending out positive vibes, then what's coming back to you is also positive—it's always a perfect match. But if you're sending out negative vibes, then what's coming back is also negative.

Make it a daily habit to love, give, forgive, and give thanks for everything now and in the future, and don't forget to throw in a little hope. Then, observe the miracles you are creating!

"Once you choose hope, everything is possible."

—Christopher Reeves

Q&A Cognition 13

1. The reason why I put so many famous quotes at the beginning of this Cognition is due to their potential to help create miracles in your life! Read and study each quote at the beginning of Cognition 13. Think about how you can apply each of these daily to create a better life for you and others.

2. Q: Why is it important to keep your inner world—your mental universe—predominantly loving, giving, forgiving, and full of gratitude and hope?
   A: Because the closer we are to the God-Frequency, the easier it will be for us to interact with the *Invisible Architect* and achieve our desires. Remember, your inner world creates your outer world!

3. Q: What is the real importance of practicing forgivingness?
   A: Forgiving is mainly for *your* mindset benefit and spiritual development so you can free up your personal energy from toxic emotions.

4. Q: What is the miracle of giving?
   A: It is a miracle as it is the beginning of our transformation into higher beings! Giving is God-like!

5. Q: What is this thing called love?
   A: Besides being a great jazz standard, love is becoming one with the person, place, or thing being loved! It is the Be in the Be-Do-Have sequence. When you are one with something, you are *being* it. When cause and effect become one, manifestation is complete—you are in the zone!

6. Q: What is the value of practicing gratitude?
   A: A grateful mind is a happy one! Since we established that no two thoughts can be thought of simultaneously, the more often your mind is filled with gratefulness, the happier and

more optimistic you are. Gratitude is the most powerful prayer you can say and helps you perceive the world from a positive mindset, and that is a miracle!

7. Q: Why is hope life-giving?
   A: Without hope there really is no quality of life—just darkness! Hope is not wishful thinking. It's a viewpoint that despite life's challenges and misfortunes, all will work out! There is something else beyond this moment of apparent darkness!

8. Q: How can you create miracles in your daily life?
   A: Make it a daily habit to love, forgive, give, and express thanks for everything! And don't forget to go to your personal pharmacy and take your hope pill in times of need. Use the Law of Thought Substitution—it's free!

Next Cognition…

Cognition 14
Personal Growth & Development

"There is nothing noble in being superior to your fellow man; true nobility is being superior to your former self."

—*Ernest Hemingway*

"Every moment of one's existence, one is growing into more or retreating into less."

—*Norman Mailer*

Personal growth & development is a $10 billion industry! Why?

Because success is elusive, and most know that self-improvement is the key to creating the better life that they and everyone else desires. Everyone wants to achieve prosperity, have better relationships and more love in their life, and achieve greater success and happiness, but most of us are not willing to do the work to create this better life. We have become a *quick-fix society*.

We therefore seek help in the form of e-books and audiobooks, online courses, podcasts, mastermind groups, webinars, self-help apps, and one-on-one coaching.

The bottom line is that personal growth and development refers to those activities that improve a person's talents, potential, employability, relationships, time management, consciousness, and ability to realize dreams and create wealth.

Analogy: If your personal dreams are the fruit at the top of the tree of life, then personal growth would be the ladder you would need to get to the top to pick the fruit! That said, finding and climbing this ladder and earning the right to pick and experience this life-changing nutritious fruit is on you. You can cheat and hire someone to do this for you, or cut the tree down, or have a helicopter lower you from above, etc., but for some reason, the fruit will not release its treasure! It's almost as if it knows you didn't earn the life-changing knowledge it has. Apparently, the way the miracle of life is set up is that we each have our own path to walk, our own tree of knowledge to find, climb, pick, and consume the life-giving fruit as well as applying that knowledge to our lives and hopefully sharing it with others!

This book, for example, is a personal growth book, as it shares my journey: finding and climbing my tree and learning the spiritual mechanics of achieving my personal desires—the fruit at the top of the tree of life.

If you recall, spiritual mechanics is understanding the relationship between the Universal Consciousness, yourself, and its creations and the interactions thereof.

Personal spiritual growth, then, from my perspective is about becoming aware of the *Invisible Architect* and learning how to employ it consciously and efficiently in your life to manifest your desires.

Here's an applicable quote:

"God helps those who help themselves" is a motto that emphasizes the importance of self-initiative and agency. The expression is still famous around the world and used to inspire people to self-help. The phrase originated in ancient Greece and may originally have been proverbial. It is illustrated by two of Aesop's Fables, and a similar sentiment is found in ancient Greek drama. Although it has been commonly attributed to Benjamin Franklin, the modern English wording appears earlier in Algernon Sidney's work.[45]

That said…

a) Becoming aware of the *Invisible Architect* can be difficult, as it is subtle and invisible, making it almost impossible to tune in to, given life's distractions and survival challenges.

b) It takes concentration and the raising of your frequency to give and receive communication to and from the Architect.

c) It takes personal work, faith, gratitude, and patience for the desire to be fulfilled.

Becoming aware of the *Invisible Architect* and the spiritual mechanics necessary to efficiently interact with it is not a quick fix! As mentioned, it takes study, work, and application. But once you achieve this awareness, you will be amazed how, by simply inviting the *Invisible Architect* to express itself through you, your perfect Divine life within will begin manifesting!

Repeat this affirmation every night upon retiring and every morning upon awakening and/or when feeling down and observe your growth:

"Perfect life within me (perfect life being the Invisible Architect), come forth into expression through me of that which I am and lead me ever into the paths of perfection causing me to see only the good; and by this process, the soul shall be illumined, acquainted with God (the *Invisible Architect*) and shall be at peace." —Ernest Holmes with clarification.

---

[45]Algernon Sidney, or Sydney, (1623-1683) was a republican political theorist. The works of Algernon Sidney, along with those of contemporary John Locke are considered a cornerstone of Western thought. Sidney directly opposed the Divine right of kings political theory by suggesting ideas such as limited government, the voluntary consent of the people, and the right of citizens to alter or abolish a corrupt government. *Discourses Concerning Government* has been called "the textbook of the American revolution."

Note: Pay very close attention to any new thoughts, ideas, people entering your life, dreams, gut feelings, hunches, coincidences… whatever. This affirmation is a powerful invitation to the *Invisible Architect*, the perfect life within you that is in all of us, to begin expressing its perfection through you!

And be consistent! The *Invisible Architect* awaits your invitation. Do it every day and every night as directed and watch what happens!

Remember, your general success in this dimension is in direct proportion to your spiritual and personal growth. There should be a natural constant urge to get better in all areas. A lack of drive to get better is usually due to past desires having never manifested as intended. We could call this *failure*. But there really is no such thing as failure; there's giving up, which should never be an option!

Remember, throughout the entire universe the Law of Cause and Effect is ever at work. This law is supreme; first there is a cause and then there is an effect. They can never operate independently. Their congruence is a must; if not—if the desired effect is lacking—then the original cause is lacking. Cause and effect are twin conditions.

If a desire has failed to manifest, there is a bug somewhere in the Be + Do = Have formula.

So, to manifest the desire that was thwarted, locate it and re-energize it by re-envisioning the original desire until you are again excited about it! This simply means to repetitively put your attention—thought energy—back on it; take your attention off the "failure" (really just a temporary delay and an opportunity to learn) and any considerations and evaluations you have connected with it, as that is the non-optimum desire, the unwanted effect.

Remember that to change any unwanted effect (condition in the outer world), one must change its cause (condition in the inner world). This is the Law of Correspondence or, stated in a different way, the Law of Cause and Effect: inner world equals outer world; subjective universe creates objective universe; thoughts create reality; your seed (desire) becomes planted in your subconscious garden and with imagination and expectation, you allow it to become that which it is in the garden of reality!

In summary, personal growth must be spiritual in nature. It is the ongoing process of understanding spiritual mechanics—your relationship between the *Invisible Architect* and its creations and the interactions thereof—and developing yourself in order to achieve your fullest potential. Personal growth and development is a vital part in your growth, maturity, success, and happiness. It is the foundation of emotional, physical, intellectual, and spiritual health.

Q&A Cognition 14

1. Q: If your personal desires are the fruit at the top of a tall tree, then what would personal growth and development be?
   A: It would be the ladder or the way for you to get to the top of the tree to pick the fruit—become aware of the *Invisible Architect* and achieve your desires!

2. Q: Is there a way to get to the top of the tree by cheating and not doing the work to personally grow and develop mentally and spiritually?
   A: No! Even if you temporarily get to the top of the tree with no work, the fruit will not release its nutritious knowledge!

3. Q: What does the motto "God helps those who help themselves" mean?
   A: It emphasizes the importance of self-initiative and agency. Sitting on a cloud and envisioning your desire and doing nothing is not a successful activity.

4. Q: Is just becoming aware of the *Invisible Architect* all that is necessary to design your life from within?
   A: No, absolutely not! This is not a quick fix—it takes study, work, and the application of knowledge and principles. But once you achieve this awareness, you will be amazed how, by simply inviting the *Invisible Architect* to express itself through you, your perfect Divine life within will begin manifesting!

5. Memorize and repeat this affirmation every night upon retiring and upon rising and observe your spiritual growth:
   "Perfect life within me, come forth into expression through me of that which I am and lead me ever into the paths of perfection causing me to see only the good; and by this process, the soul shall be illumined, acquainted with God and shall be at peace."—Ernest Holmes

6. Q: What does your general success in this plane of existence depend upon?
    A: Your success is in direct proportion to your spiritual and personal growth.

7. Q: If you are failing at achieving any desire, what is the reason?
    A: There's always a reason—a bug somewhere in the Be + Do = Have formula.

8. Q: What's the process, then, to achieve that desire that is not manifesting?
    A: Re-energize it by restating it as a goal already achieved until you become excited about it again. Get rid of any negative thoughts you have about not having manifested it yet (use thought substitution if necessary). Remember, to change any unwanted situation, you must first change its cause in your inner world.

9. Q: What really is personal growth?
    A: Personal growth must be spiritual in nature. It's an ongoing process not only for understanding your relationship with the *Invisible Architect* but also for developing yourself to your fullest potential. Personal growth is the foundation of your emotional, physical, intellectual, and spiritual health.

Next Cognition…

Cognition 15
Life Is for Lessons

"There are no mistakes in life, only lessons. There is no such thing as a negative experience, only opportunities to grow, learn and advance along the road of self-mastery."

—*Robin Sharma*

"The only real mistake is the one from which we learn nothing."

—*John Powel*

"Every calamity is a spur and a valuable hint."

—*Emerson*

When you have a problem and cannot think of a solution, that does not mean that one doesn't exist, especially if you know the spiritual mechanics of employing the all-knowing *Invisible Architect*!

Finding a solution the hard way often starts with defining a clear goal and then, step by step, identifying and peeling off the problems you observe in your outer world that inhibit your reaching it. This is somewhat workable but not permanent.

Or you can put your energy and attention on your inner world, as has been discussed throughout my Cognitions, and delegate the *Invisible Architect* to assist you in solving all problems associated with your achieving your outer-world desire. I call this working smarter, not harder! Why? Because the *Invisible Architect* has way more knowledge and causative resources to plan, advise, reorganize, and coordinate everything in the Intelligent Energy Field, where all solutions already exist to attract the problem-solving people and situations to manifest your desires in ways you could never imagine! (See my stories in Cognition 2 for examples.)

What I'm saying is that real solutions do not really exist in the real world; they are mental constructs. They do not readily present themselves in our minds (inner world) unless they are stated as a goal redefined—present-time affirmations of the desire already achieved. (See Cognition 8.)

The question then becomes two-fold: where do these desires and problems come from, and what is their purpose other than keeping us busy with life's challenges?

I believe life is for lessons.

A life lesson is just what it sounds like—a lesson learned while living life. It's really based on the idea of learning from experience and especially from your mistakes. These lessons could be described as defining moments that are remembered. Since they are based on an individual's life experiences, they are unique to each person.

And maybe there is no right or wrong choice and no good or bad path, only choices that eventually lead to the lessons you need to learn at *that* time in your life. Once you learn the lessons, maybe you'll start making different choices in the future, which, of course, *is* your choice!

I believe this was the plot of the movie *Groundhog Day*, starring Bill Murray. Murray played the part of a cynical TV weatherman who finds himself reliving the same day repeatedly when he goes on location to the small town of Punxsutawney to film a report about their annual Groundhog Day. His predicament drives him to distraction, until he sees a way of turning the situation to his advantage.

Perhaps you have chronic non-optimum situations in your life. No matter what you do, these problems seem to keep repeating themselves to no end—e.g., struggles with money, career, health, relationships, etc. A fresh point of view might help you solve them, the point of view being asking yourself some questions:

- "Is there a lesson to be learned here?"
- "Am I missing out on an opportunity?"
- "What is *my* responsibility for this problem's existence?"
- "Is the *Invisible Architect* trying to tell me something, but I'm not listening?"

Remember, any real-world situation must have a corresponding cause that is manifesting this effect. If you have a desire that has been achieved, then bravo! Your goal redefined has manifested. But if you are having a "Groundhog Day" situation, you must change the *cause* to match the wanted *effect*. Maybe, for example, you are continually having relationship issues. Your desire is to find a soulmate, but every new relationship eventually fails. You're starting to feel cursed and unlucky.

Per the Law of Cause and Effect, there must be some counter-thought to that original desire.

Maybe, for example, your stated desire is to have a great soulmate to spend the rest of your life with. Per the Be-Do-Have sequence, you redefine that goal, affirming it in the now as "I have a great soulmate to spend the rest of my life with." But deep in your subconscious is the thought "I'll never have a great soulmate relationship. I'll end up lonely like my father," or some negative thought like that. Whichever statement is predominant will determine the outer-world manifestation. That produces infinite possibilities, given the variables.

It's best therefore to immediately use the Law of Thought Substitution, which states that no two thoughts can be active simultaneously. So, every time that negative thought or belief enters your personal universe, you restate it with faith and expectation. "I have a great soulmate to spend the rest of my life with." You affirm this ideal result, especially at night while in the hypnagogic state, in the morning upon awakening, and every time doubts and reservations enter your mental space.

Learning and applying this thought substitution process puts you back at being causative, in the driver's seat, versus being a passenger, which is being more of a victim—part of the effect, not the cause. It will make it easier to affirm and manifest your original desire if you don't allow yourself to be distracted by the negative counter thoughts that we all experience.

The question then becomes, "Who is creating these problems that need solutions from which lessons can be learned?"

The answer to this is the solution to any problem—you! You are the cause, the Be in the Be-Do-Have Sequence.

You, a Spirit with a unique energy signature, created by the Great Spirit (*Invisible Architect*) and therefore of the same nature, bring goals (desires) into existence, which in return create problems to be solved in the Physical Universe to manifest these desires, correct?

Based upon my observations and experiences already discussed, the Spirit itself creates problems it wishes to solve for the purpose of learning lessons and knowing itself. To most, this statement will be hard to digest, but it's true![46]

Physicists have various theories regarding this, the Big Bang theory being the prevailing cosmological one. Under this theory, space and time emerged together 13.799 ± 0.021 billion years ago, and the energy and

---

[46]Speculation: This is the same process I believe that the Invisible Architect used to create the Universe and everything in it, including you and me. The Invisible Architect, for whatever reasons, postulated a desire and with its powers solved all the problems necessary to create that desire—a miracle we call the Physical Universe and life!

matter initially present have become less dense as the Universe has expanded.[47]

Q: Well okay…but who or what created this event?
A: The *Invisible Architect*, which always was and always will be.

Note: I have asked the *Invisible Architect* this question, and the answer I have received is the information in this book, which I was told to share.

Remember the Thomas Troward datum from Cognition 6:

"I am the person that thou art; thou art the person that I am."

Continual alternating between these two positions is the Ultimate Truth, and as Troward says in his book *The Hidden Power*," The Truth shall set you free."

The Law of Attraction (Cause and Effect) is always working, so you'd better use *focused prayer*, which is defined as asking the Intelligent Energy Field that permeates all things and that you are a part of to express itself through you. (See Cognition 9).

It is therefore especially important to get control over your thoughts and beliefs, or they will control you, and your life will manifest undesirable situations. Then, you will likely tend to blame these situations on everybody and everything other than you!

Why continue *your* Groundhog Day when you can shorten and even end it?!

Summary:

Goals create problems, which need solutions.

These solutions are best discovered through the Be-Do-Have Sequence.

---

[47] Universe. Wikipedia, the free encyclopedia.

Be (Inner World): This is assuming the beingness of the problem solved while *feeling* the reality of the state sought using your Divine gift of imagination.

Do (Manifestation Process): This sets in motion the manifestation process by your personal Individual Architect along with your proactivity and support.

Have (Outer World): Advance gratitude or being grateful in the now for the desire or wish you want fulfilled in the future. Neville Goddard in his book *The Power of Imagination* calls this "thinking from the end."

Q&A Cognition 15

1. Q: When it comes to manifesting your desires, what does it mean to work smarter rather than harder?
   A: The hard way is to define your goal and then, step by step, identify and peel off each problem you observe in reality—your outer world—that inhibit reaching it. It would be smarter to simply put your attention first on your inner world using the Be-Do-Have sequence previously discussed and delegate the solution to a Superior Intelligence (*Invisible Architect*) to assist you in the manifesting process.

2. Q: What is a life lesson?
   A: It's a lesson you learn while living life! It's based on the idea of learning from experience, especially your mistakes. Since they are based on an individual's life experiences, they are unique to each person.

3. Q: What is the solution to any lifestyle situation?
   A: You! You are the cause, the Be in the Be + Do = Have sequence.

4. Q: Who then creates problems for the purpose of learning lessons?
   A: Each unique spirit is created by the Great Spirit (*Invisible Architect*), and therefore is of the same nature. We postulate desires into existence, which in return create problems to be solved in the Physical Universe to manifest these desires.

5. Q: Why is it important to get control over your thoughts and beliefs?
   A: Because if you don't, they will control you and begin manifesting undesirable outer world situations! The Law of Attraction is always in play.

6. Q: What does "I am the person that thou art; thou art the person that I am" mean?
   A: It means you and the *Invisible Architect* are ONE; you are both Spirit! Just as an actor can change characters at will, you can alternate between the character of *you*, the individual spirit(particular*)*, and the character of *you*, the *Invisible Architect*(absolute). This is THE secret to manifestation, as when you "BE-come" the *Invisible Architect*, your thoughts are empowered to create anything! Go into the Silence and meditate on this.

7. Q: Explain briefly the Be + Do = Have manifestation process.
   A: Assume the beingness of the desire to be achieved (solved) and envision what it would *feel* like using your Divine gift of imagination if achieved (solved). This sets in motion your personal Individual Architect along with your supported proactivity. To ensure manifestation, express gratefulness in the present for the desire or wish already fulfilled. This is called advance gratitude.

Next Cognition…

Cognition 16
The Architect's Message

"All I have seen teaches me to trust the Creator for all I have not seen."
—*Ralph Waldo Emerson*

"The greatest discovery of any generation is that a human can alter his life by altering his attitude."
—*William James*

The experience I have had and continue to have on my personal journey is like the one told in James Redfield's bestselling novel *The Celestine Prophecy*. The book is a first-person narrative of spiritual awakening. The narrator is in a transitional period of his life and begins to notice instances of synchronicity, which are coincidences that have a meaning personal to those who experience them. This book discusses various psychological and spiritual ideas that are rooted in many ancient Eastern traditions, such as how being open to new possibilities can help an individual establish a connection with the Divine. In hindsight, that's exactly what happened to me when I was three years old and made my first knowing contact with my "inner voice," which, unbeknownst to me, started my personal journey and interactions with the Divine—the

Invisible Architect. And just as the narrator of *The Celestine Prophecy* learned "insights," one by one, during his personal journey, so did I have "cognitions" from my experiences and insights. And they continue to this day and will continue, I'm sure, beyond!

These experiences and synchronicities for me are empirical evidence of our connection to the Divine—the validation of the existence of an intelligent energy we are not only all connected to but can employ to design our lives and create a better world. And just as gravity is invisible but observable and follows certain laws, this mystical Intelligence is invisible and observable and follows certain laws, as evidence of my personal interactions have previously mentioned. You may wish to name this Universal Energy something more personal to you, which is why I have shared many of the names I use…your choice!

I did not write this book as an attempt to prove the existence of this Intelligence. I am not a scientist, physicist, or philosopher. I am a musician/composer/author who simply had the urge to share his experiences and hard-earned knowledge regarding the subject of spiritual mechanics—the relationship between the Universal Consciousness and its creations and the interactions thereof.

In 2019, if you recall, my new single "Good to Go" achieved number one on the Contemporary Jazz Billboard Charts. It was my first number one and quite a musical career win! Shortly thereafter I received the following inner voice message from the *Invisible Architect*:

"John, you now need to spread the WORD!"

Startled and confused, I said, "What WORD?"

My inner voice answered, "That everybody is a spiritual being and can use this supernatural bodyguard and consultant—the Architect—to help design their lives and contribute to a better world; and that there are fundamentals that once learned will contribute greatly to this end."

I wrestled with the message for several months, but the resultant urge felt more like a duty, and so I began the writing in September 2019. The interesting thing is that it almost feels like I'm not the author but more of an assistant author and/or translator for the *Invisible Architect* to express itself, as crazy as that sounds. The reason I say this is as I began writing down my personal experiences, my mind began flooding with the overall outline and details…so much so that I had to stop, organize, and sort through these thoughts. I smiled and could see that the book was just about going to write itself, which validated even more that it was my duty to write it.

Like thoughts attract like thoughts…

Invisible Architect Fundamentals

- The *Invisible Architect* is all-love, all-beauty, infinite intelligence, omniscience, omnipotence, and all-wisdom.
- All of us have a Divine purpose, and it's up to each of us while living life to discover this purpose through our personal growth, knowledge, and experience.
- The Intelligent Energy Field, the *Invisible Architect*, knows itself by expressing itself through its creations, specifically through each of our Divine purposes and desires.
- The *Invisible Architect* can only do this if we invite it to do so. This is crucial!
- We have freedom of choice in this matter, which I find interesting and refreshing, as that adds self-determinism to the matrix.
- Just as the *Invisible Architect* has the power to create by thought, so do we, as we are of the same nature, being one of its creations.
- All thoughts are creative and by their nature can and do create realities.
- And just as the *Invisible Architect* knows itself through its creations, we know ourselves through *our* creations, which are as well accomplished by creative thought.
- The Law of Cause and Effect is impersonal and neutral—neither good nor evil, moral nor immoral.
- Your conscious mind is the objective or thinking mind given to us by the Creator that uses our senses to perceive and analyze. It is the interface between you and your subconscious or subjective

mind—the particular of the absolute Quantum Energy Field that permeates all.

- Our subconscious mind is the communication portal to the *Invisible Architect*.

- If you think good. Good actions follow, and good realities are created.

- If you think evil, evil actions follow, and evil realities are created.

- To change any undesirable reality, reaffirm the desired reality as completed in the present (goal redefined) and continue the Be-Do-Have affirmation process.

- Unless acted upon adversely (negative thoughts or beliefs counter to the original desire), a clear dominant desire (seed) planted into the subconscious immediately starts, even if ever so slowly, evolving into that desire being fulfilled per the Law of Growth. The speed with which this occurs is proportional to your understanding and use of the spiritual mechanics involved—the ambition and strength of your desire, the strength of any counter-thoughts, if any, your handling of these counter-thoughts, and your persistence and patience!

- Counter-thoughts to any desire can interrupt, modify, slow down, and/or stop that desire's manifestation proportionate to their power and consistency.

- Patience is not only a virtue but also critical in interacting with the *Invisible Architect*, given the difference in our personal thought universe and the dense frequency Physical Universe. Manifestation in the Physical Universe can happen quickly or can take time, given the nature and magnitude of our desires and/or our effective or ineffective application of the spiritual mechanics involved. It also depends upon patience, as impatience can sabotage our manifestations.

This might be best understood by relaying the story of the Chinese bamboo tree.

The Story of the Chinese Bamboo Tree

Like with any plant, the growth of the Chinese bamboo tree requires nurturing—water, fertile soil, sunshine. In its first year, we see no visible signs of activity. In the second year, again, no growth above the soil. The third, the fourth, still nothing. Our patience is tested, and we begin to wonder if our efforts (caring, water, etc.) will ever be rewarded.

And finally, in the fifth year—behold, a miracle! We experience growth. And what growth it is! The Chinese bamboo tree grows eighty feet in just six weeks!

But let's be serious. Does the Chinese bamboo tree really grow eighty feet in six weeks? Did the Chinese bamboo tree lie dormant for four years only to grow exponentially in the fifth? Or was the little tree growing underground, developing a root system strong enough to support its potential for outward growth in the fifth year and beyond? The answer is, of course, obvious. Had the tree not developed a strong unseen foundation, it could not have sustained its life as it grew. The same principle is true for people. People who patiently toil toward worthwhile dreams and goals, building strong character while overcoming adversity and challenge, grow the strong internal foundation to handle success, while "get-rich-quickers" and lottery winners usually are unable to sustain unearned success and wealth.

Had the Chinese bamboo tree farmer dug up his little seed every year to see if it was growing, he would have stunted the Chinese bamboo tree's growth as surely as a caterpillar is doomed to a life on the ground if it is freed from its struggle inside a cocoon prematurely. The struggle in the cocoon is what gives the future butterfly the wing-power to fly!

Remember the Law of Opposites.

If you begin experiencing any pushback, use that as a sign that the Quantum Intelligent Field has been given a declaration and is in the middle of rearranging its energy, an energy where everything including your desire already exists, into your wish fulfilled.

So, smile and have patience. In the case of the bamboo tree, it only appears that there is no growth, but unseen miraculous growth is nevertheless occurring underground. Same with the manifestation process. The *Invisible Architect* has powers beyond our understanding, and if your desire has been accepted by the subconscious, there are many unseen things being orchestrated that may or may not take some time to come together. Therefore, it is not only important to continue the Be-Do-Have process as discussed, but it is also important to have patience and trust the *Invisible Architect*'s ability to manifest your desires.

This might be exceedingly difficult at first, but after a few demonstrations of its awesome power, you will be humbled and have total faith, as was the case with me.

So, let go! If you put your attention on anything negative that you are experiencing, you will slow and potentially even stop the manifestation process due to your counter-energy.

Don't dig up your implanted seed of desire prematurely!

Your thoughts, beliefs, and attitudes are that powerful because they are wired to the *Invisible Architect*, who is *always* acting upon all of them.

Once you understand this, you will master the game; but until you do, the game masters you!

I AM THAT I AM
YOU ARE WHAT YOU WILL TO BE

The *Invisible Architect* is the live wire that you, as its child, need to be aware of and hooked up to. You are the spiritual/physical representation (the particular) of the *Invisible Architect* (the absolute) and so a channel for its energy to manifest anything that *you* think with your thoughts!

When your individual mind touches the Universal Mind, you receive all the power you need to handle *any* situation! Your ability, therefore, to eliminate any imperfect condition depends on your connection to the all-perfect *Invisible Architect*!

Mental action depends upon consciousness (being aware) of this power and using it. Therefore, the more conscious you become of your unity with the *Invisible Architect*, the greater your power to control and master any condition will be.

Mental action is the interaction of the individual upon the *Invisible Architect*—the Intelligent Energy Field. And since the *Invisible Architect* is the intelligence that pervades all space and animates all living things, this mental action and reaction is the Law of Causation—the fundamental mechanics of how you manifest anything!

This is the Secret to the "Secret!"

Q&A Cognition 16

1. Q: What does this quote by Emerson mean: "All I have seen teaches me to trust the Creator for all I have not seen."?
   A: You have your own Divine Intelligence, the *Invisible Architect*, within you that is accessible to you to help you design your perfect life if you know that all thoughts and beliefs are creative and can manifest realities.

2. Q: How do I communicate with the *Invisible Architect*?
   A: Through the portal of your subconscious mind.

3. Q: What is the exact process?
   A: Using the Be + Do = Have formula previously discussed.

4. Q: We know patience is a virtue, but why is it critical in the manifestation process?
   A: Manifestation in the Physical Universe can take time a) given the density of the frequency of the Physical Universe and the nature and magnitude of our desires and b) how effective our application of the Be-Do-Have process is—i.e., the spiritual mechanics. Impatience can sabotage our manifestations. (See the story of the Chinese bamboo tree.)

5. Q: What should you do if you begin experiencing any kind of pushback in the achievement of your desire?
   A: Smile and have patience. If your stated desire is and remains clear and focused and has been repetitively planted and accepted by the *Invisible Architect*, the manifestation process is underway. This Superior Intelligence has powers beyond our understanding, and there are many unseen events and circumstances being orchestrated that may take some time to come together. Continue practicing the Law of Cause and Effect exactly as discussed earlier and trust the *Invisible Architect*'s ability to manifest your desire.

6. Q: Why is it important to be in perfect harmony with the *Invisible Architect*?

    A: Because when your individual mind touches the Universal Mind, you receive all the power you need to handle any situation. Your ability to eliminate any imperfect condition depends on your being the All-Perfect *Invisible Architect* and consciously using its power!

Next Cognition…

Cognition 17
The Connection Is the Secret!

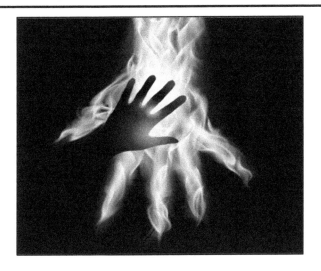

"Every man's life is a fairy tale written by God's fingers."

—*Hans Christian Andersen*

The angel number 1111 means that a spiritual presence is with you. The Divine is crossing your path and has a message to share. Often it is a nudge to become aware of the present moment.

Pay attention to the number 1111 presenting itself in your life!

Example: Today, January 11, 2020, I heard my number one hit song "Good to Go" on the radio at the exact moment I finished the first draft of my book! Talk about synchronicity! Blew me away! Then I noticed the following four number ones:

"Good to Go" = My number one hit song on the Billboard jazz chart; January = first month of 2020 (number one); Date 11th = 11!

Coincidental four ones or a Divine acknowledgment?

The Awareness of the Connection Is the Secret!

Q&A Cognition 17

1. Q: What is the significance of 1111?
   A: Repeating numbers and number sequences chained together are known as angel numbers. Angel number 1111 is supposed to be a special message from your guardian angels indicating your ability to connect with the Ascended Masters in the angelic realm. It is your connection with the angelic realm, God, or Source Energy that determines your ability to manifest your desires and achieve your full potential. Was completing my book on January 11 and hearing my number one hit song a coincidence or a message?

2. Q: Why is the connection the Secret?
   A: Because we are all unique individual intelligent energy beings created by the *Invisible Architect's* creative thought! That is the source of our power and the reason why becoming aware of our true nature—our connection to and interaction with the *Invisible Architect*—is the secret to designing our lives from within!

3. Think of all the times you felt connected to the *Invisible Architect*. How did you feel during those times? Describe in detail.

Author's Commentary
Epilogue

Your perfect life has already been achieved! It exists as unorganized energy in the Quantum Intelligent Energy Field, waiting for you to...

- **Be:** Become conscious of its existence!
- **Do:** Claim it as yours, which translates to imagining it already fulfilled!
- **Have:** Express your gratitude in advance for this Divine gift!

"Remember the future"—the process of becoming aware of and imagining your perfect future life in the now!

Hopefully, the Cognitions in this book—a book I never imagined I'd write until I realized it was my duty to write it—will help you understand the spiritual mechanics involved in inviting the *Invisible Architect* to express its Divine Word, your WORD, through you so you can design your perfect life from within!

"Life is God's novel. Let him write it."—Isaac Bashevis Singer

"Nothing can hinder your Divine life from manifesting but you! Share this with others, and together we can create a better world!

—John Novello

Addendum 1
I Am Affirmations
(Awaken Your Power)

"Whether you think you can, or you think you can't—you're right."

—*Henry Ford*

This Henry Ford quote, if put in the Be-Do-Have formula, could be summed up as:

"To Be (think you can) or not to Be (think you can't)."

"I Am or I Am Not."

Affirmations are "to be" statements!

The purpose of repetitively stating your goals as already achieved "to be" statements (affirmations) is twofold:

1. Convincing your conscious mind (you) through repetition that they are possible to achieve.

2. Implanting them into your subconscious with strong emotions and feelings, the same emotions and feelings you would naturally have when the desire was achieved!
3. Express advance gratitude *now* in the present for your not-yet-achieved outer world desires but achieved, no doubt, in your inner world!

Understanding these fundamentals is critical, as otherwise these statements are simply useless time-wasting repetitive statements.

Convincing your analytical self of achieving your desire even if you are doubtful is assisted by repetitively stating your desire as achieved. As the law seems to work, our consciousness imagines ideas and impresses them on the subconscious. The subconscious, which is related to the *Invisible Architect* in a way that I do not know—probably an individual harmonic of the Universal Subconscious—receives these ideas.

If your desire is clear and repetitively stated with intense heartfelt feeling in the present as having already been achieved, the subconscious eventually accepts it as factual and begins giving these ideas form and expression in the garden of our senses (outer world) unless otherwise redirected or alloyed by a negative counter-thought or effort.

Without this sequence, which we established earlier as the Be-Do-Have sequence, nothing is created and exists. This could be called the Law of Consciousness, as all things evolve out of consciousness (awareness) of existence.

So, once you are convinced of your goal being achieved, then you continue to believe and act that it indeed *has* been achieved until it has been perfectly expressed in the Physical Universe—the universe of perception (consciousness). The arbitrary of time that exists in the dense lower-frequency Physical Universe is what creates pushback—doubt and counter-thought—because your physical perceptions are not yet conscious (aware) of the desire's arrival.

In other words, the stated desire is perfect in your inner world, but the expression of the desire in your outer world is subject to the Law of Growth, which takes time in the physical dimension.

In your personal universe, if you have followed the theory of the exercise correctly, it should already clearly exist! So, the trick is to not agree with your objective reality that says, "Sorry, you can state your desire until you're blue in the face, but it does not exist here. Your statement is a lie." Ignore that pushback because it is false!

It may not have fully manifested *yet* due to the arbitrary of time (the Law of Growth), but its archetype has already been created—created and imagined with the same exciting feeling you would have if it were already achieved—in the Quantum Intelligent Energy Field and has been scheduled for delivery to the universe of perceptions contingent to your declaration!

You therefore need to be home to accept delivery, okay?

So per the Be-Do-Have process, first you Be-come it. You then Be-come *conscious (aware)* of it. And then you continue to Be-come conscious (aware) of it *until* that which you have been *being* conscious of manifests in the Physical Universe.

So, once you declare your desired realty as already achieved in the now (goal redefined), the only reason there's a lag in the dense lower-frequency Physical Universe is contingent to time and to your proper use of the Law of Cause and Effect. When you think about it, this is a good thing, as it wouldn't be much of a game and learning experience if everything we imagined instantly manifested; in fact, it would probably be downright dangerous!

Remember…without a clarity of the desire already achieved (faith) accompanied by a dominant feeling of the desire being achieved in your life—what that would mean to your life, in other words—the subconscious doesn't readily accept it, let alone begin the process of reorganizing the Intelligent Energy Field into your desire fulfilled.

Analogy: You can't plant seed in infertile soil—it won't take root (be accepted)!

This is the Law of Attraction, Cause & Effect and/or Correspondence.

Summary:

If you affirm with clarity and certainty-of-belief your goal as completed in the present and then add a strong feeling and burning desire to achieve it, which makes an impression on the subconscious, then unless acted on by a more powerful feeling of an opposite nature (counter-feeling), it *must* manifest.

What you feel you are (Be) always dominates what you feel you would like to be. That's why desires should be redefined in the present instead of as a goal that has the element of time as a criterion.

To *be* is stronger than thinking you will be.

To feel you *will be* is to admit you are not.

To feel that you *are* is stronger than you are not.

The following powerful affirmations should be affirmed as follows:

1. Repetitively affirm, either out loud or in thought, every night while in the hypnagogic state until you fall asleep.
2. If you wake up for any reason, repeat #1.
3. Repeat #1 in the morning when you awake and before you get out of bed.
4. Repeat #1 during the day whenever you get a minute. (Note: Although you are not in the hypnagogic state, this still acts as a reminder to your conscious and subconscious and maintains the dominant thought.)
5. Each time you repeat the process, feel the reality of the state desired and live and act on that conviction until the miracle manifests (Be and Do).

6. Also express advance gratitude for your desire's manifestation, even though your physical senses say otherwise.
7. Continue this process until your desire manifests, and then give real thanks, the likes of which you have never given before!

And remember the story of the Chinese bamboo plant—be patient!

Affirmations: Goals Redefined

Note: You can and should create your own precise personal affirmations on any non-optimum big or small situation—money, love, personal relations, career, health, house, car, clothes, stress, worry, jealousy, anger management, migraines—any non-optimum situation.

Since earning and having money for one's needs is important, as an abundance of it solves many life situations and money is a great source of frustration and struggle, I have provided a list of money affirmations in their proper format for your practical daily use.

Training: Each affirmation is in the form of your stated WORD (desire) and then your declaration of that WORD announced with *feeling* and *gratitude* to the *Invisible Architect* for manifestation.

The power of I AM. I AM is the WORD of God; if *you* state it, it is *your* WORD!

"I am" and "I am not" is a goal redefined in the now or present time, the original desire or goal being "to Be or not to Be."

Example: To be happy or not to be happy translates as a goal redefined into "I am happy" or "I am not happy!" Obviously, "I am" is more desirable than "I am not" in this example.

"I AM THAT I AM" are the words that God spoke when Moses asked for God's name in the book of Exodus in the Old Testament. So, we could simply state as an affirmation "I am (Desired Goal); I am!" (Declaring it accomplished!)

Formula:

I AM [desire], I AM!

Example:

I am happy; I am!

"I am" is *your* WORD, THE WORD, your declaration!

"In the beginning was the Word, and the Word was with God, and the Word was God."—John 1:1

Adjust your declaration "I am" to its appropriate conjugation and congruency. See below:

Money Affirmations:

"The man who owns all he wants for the living of all the life he is capable of living is rich; and no man who has not plenty of money can have all he wants and needs."—Wallace D. Wattles, *The Science of Getting Rich*

It is our right to be wealthy. We are here to lead an abundant and successful life. Look around. Abundance is all around you! We should, therefore, have all the money we need to lead a happy and prosperous life. We should view money as a symbol of exchange. If you had a physical disease, you would normally seek help as soon as you became aware of the symptoms. You would know something's wrong. Likewise, if you do not have enough money circulating in your life, you should also be thinking something is radically wrong with your exchange! Poverty, therefore, could be thought of as somewhat a mental disease.

Per the Law of Cause and Effect, we now know we can change any undesired effect in our outer world by changing the cause in our inner world that is causing that effect. This is what is meant by the phrase "designing your life from within."

Here is a partial list of declarations that should be inputted into your subconscious—I call them "money antibiotics" to the disease called "lack or scarcity of money. "As previously mentioned, the first statement is the desire stated as a goal redefined in the now; the second statement is your declaration to the Physical Universe of your wish fulfilled!

Money Antibiotics: Desire Declaration

- Dollars want me; they do!
- Money and I are friends; they are!
- I am a magnet for money; I am!
- Prosperity is drawn to me; it is!
- Money comes to me in expected and unexpected ways; it does!
- I have an abundance mindset; I do!
- I am ready to be rich; I am!
- I am worthy of making more money; I am!
- I am open and receptive to all the wealth life offers me; I am!
- I embrace new avenues of income; I do!
- I welcome an unlimited source of income and wealth in my life; I do!
- I have a lavish, steady, and dependable income consistent with integrity and mutual benefit; I do!
- I release all negative energy over money; I do!
- Money comes to me easily and effortlessly; it does!
- I use money to better my life and the lives of others; I do!
- Wealth constantly flows into my life; it does!
- Money is forever circulating in my life; it is!
- I have a supply of money for every demand; I do!
- My actions create constant prosperity; they do!
- I am aligned with the energy of abundance; I am!
- I constantly attract opportunities that create more money; I do!
- My finances improve beyond my dreams; they do!
- Money is the root of joy and comfort; it is!
- Money and spirituality can co-exist in harmony; they can!
- Money and love can be friends; they can!
- Money is my servant; it is!
- I am the master of my wealth; I am!

- I can handle large sums of money; I can!
- I am at peace with having a lot of money; I am!
- I can handle massive success with grace; I can!
- Money expands my life's opportunities and experiences; it does!
- Money creates positive impact in my life; it does!
- Money allows me to be, do, and have what I desire; it does!
- I love my positive, happy, abundant life; I do!
- God is my supply, and my supply is infinite; it is!

You can pick any subject area, big or small, that you are having trouble with and write your own affirmations accordingly.

Examples: Your career, relationships, job, family, health, happiness, self-esteem, confidence, talent, procrastination, fear of failure, work ethic, self-discipline, punctuality, responsibility, etc.

Use the money affirmation list as a guide to start creating lists in any subject area.

Tip: If you're starting a new list, I would make the first affirmation on the list an "I AM" type statement and proceed from there.

Examples:

- **Health:** I am healthy; I am!
- **Work Ethic:** I have a great work ethic; I do!
- **Punctuality:** I am always punctual; I am!
- **Family:** I have a wonderful family; I do!
- **Career:** I have a great and expanding career; I do!

Be creative and have fun!

Tip: I suggest recording these affirmations in your voice with *emotion* and *feeling* so you can listen to them while you fall asleep!

Final Prayer[48]

I promise to distribute the WORD, the WORD being that God is LOVE and that Love is in each of us; God is with us and guides us and surrounds us with his perfect peace. I thank you for my Divine gifts, especially my Divine body—the temple for you to express yourself, the WORD—through me as that which I am. Please forgive me my bad deeds and actions, as I forgive those who commit bad deeds and actions against me and deliver me from all incorrect thinking.

It is now time for me to claim what is mine and do the work I was sent here to do—namely, to use my Divine gifts to serve and inspire others, thereby creating a lavish and dependable income, allowing me the opportunity to distribute the WORD!

With great gratitude and respect...

[Your name]

---

[48]Please read daily, especially before retiring and upon rising, in order to assure acceptance by your subconscious mind.

Addendum 2

Designing Your Life

"There is one quality which one must possess to win, and that is definiteness of purpose, the knowledge of what one wants, and a burning desire to possess it."

—Napoleon Hill

Employing the *Invisible Architect* and the Law of Cause and Effect to design your life from within places you in the driver's seat of your own life. Your outer world will be a direct reflection of your inner world when you accept full responsibility for your inner life. This takes you out of the victim role, making you the sole creator of your own life—the end of self-imposed spiritual slavery!

That said, if you have postulated (affirmed) a desired reality but it has not manifested accordingly, then there is a bug somewhere in the process.

Exercise #1: Failed Desires (Undesired Reality)

Theory: Since cause (Be) and effect (Have) are twins per the Law of Correspondence, that means that any undesired reality in your outer world has a corresponding cause in your inner world, per the Be-Do-Have formula. Therefore, to change the undesired reality, you *must* change the cause (Be) that is manifesting the undesired reality (Have).

Procedure:

1. Write down every non-optimum outer world situation, starting from the most urgent and then biggest to smallest. (This is taking inventory.) These are your desires that failed or are failing to manifest properly.

2. Now state each one of these non-optimum situations (failed or failing desires) as optimum situations (achieved desires).

3. Pick the most urgent desire needing to be manifested and imagine with *intense feeling* and *burning desire* that it is completed in your inner world. Imagine this desire completed before retiring, upon awakening, and daily as is needed through repetitive thought, spoken word, and/or even a recording of your own voice stating this goal redefined as a completed statement. Note: If you make a recording in your own voice, I suggest falling asleep listening to it with earphones on. Record it multiple times for at least an hour. This hour of work will be well spent, as you will be able to use it repeatedly every night, planting this desire into your subconscious mind.

4. If you receive any negative counter-thoughts from your mind, others, or any outside source, apply the Law of Thought Substitution as described earlier and replace that counter-thought with the original declaration ASAP! Keep doing this until you become master over the dream thief's attempts to alloy your WORD!

5. Give advance gratitude as if it has already been achieved by you!

Suggestion: Make a recording in your own voice repetitively thanking the *Invisible Architect* in advance for manifesting this desire! This recording should be thirty to sixty minutes long and express gratitude for your desire achieved and how wonderful your life is in every aspect. Use your imagination. Then with headphones on, listen to the recording every night as you fall asleep. This process will plant this desire as already fulfilled into your subconscious mind. (Note: You can make one recording that includes both the imagining of the desire achieved and your advance gratitude.)

Remember…once you convince your subconscious of this desire achieved through repetition and added feeling and burning desire, that's when the fireworks begin—only then. So, have patience.

But what really is a "burning desire"?

Imagine you are scuba diving about fifty feet underwater and something goes wrong with your oxygen supply. You quickly go through your training checklist, but nothing is working. You're out of time. You need oxygen now. It's life or death! You start to quickly head to the surface with what little breath you have left, but you notice an ominous killer great white shark above. What do you do? You would normally hide and wait for the danger to pass, but you can't! You need oxygen now, and you'll have to risk a possible shark attack and get to the surface at all costs!

That is burning desire, and without it nothing great ever gets accomplished!

So, on a scale of desire, ten being burning desire and one being it would be nice to maybe achieve one day, assess your desires, big and small. Where are you at on this burning desire scale regarding each desire?

For example, say you have a desire, as I did, to make a living as a jazz pianist and composer. Simply stated, this is "I am a successful jazz pianist/composer." Well, is that a pipe dream (a one on the burning desire scale), or is it "I will get to the surface at all costs or die trying" (a ten)? Well, I'll tell you...considering it took twenty-five years of practice to develop my talent and craft and another ten years to become competitive and achieve my musical career goals, it is a good thing it wasn't a pipe dream for me, as I would have given up a long time ago.

In his book *Rhinoceros Success*, Scott Alexander uses a rhinoceros as the symbol for charging full speed toward every opportunity! You wake up every morning as a full-grown, six-thousand-pound rhino, get out of bed like a thick-skinned, unstoppable rhino (not a sloth), take a quick shower, brush your horns, put your rhino clothes on, get mad, and charge!

I mean, who is going to argue with an irritable, disgusted, angry, three-ton rhinoceros? You *will* get what you want. Vow never to go back to that pasture with your lazy cow buddies. Just charge ahead after your desire!

And just so there's no mis-estimation of effort, that's what it takes—an unstoppable burning desire! Do you think a mad, charging rhinoceros cares if you're pointing a powerful big game rifle at him? No! And you'd better not miss your shot because he's coming!

The best way to create the proper feeling necessary to impress your desire on your subconscious is to close your eyes and imagine the Be, Do, and Have of your desire after having achieved it in the garden of the senses—Physical Universe, your outer world. Imagine who you would be; what you now would be able to do; what your close friends would be doing, thinking and saying; what you would have that you don't have now. In other words, imagine your changed new life in as much detail as is necessary to put a big smile on your face, to be excited, to feel like you would probably feel when your desire manifests!

Here's a personal side story:

I can remember when I was going through some tough times due to a lack of money. I was not only poor, but I was also *being* poor in my own mind, my inner world. I would walk into the grocery store and avoid the steak section because I knew I couldn't afford it. I was not only Being broke but I was acting (Doing) broke! I had contracted the disease of poverty. But one day, I was walking out of the grocery store with a few inexpensive chicken legs (they weren't even from the more expensive organic section). I had an epiphany about this, and so I experimented with being affluent, not broke. I imagined with feeling, as the drill suggests, who I would be and what I would be doing and having if my desire of being affluent had been achieved. I almost made it to my car when my mindset changed to an affluent one. My mental antibiotics kicked in. So, what do you think happened next? You guessed it. I went back into the grocery store and bought a twenty-five-dollar New York steak with the remaining money on my almost maxed credit card and cooked a great steak dinner that I'll never forget! It was the beginning of changing my consciousness of lack and scarcity to one of affluence. Some of you may view this as being irresponsible, but in fact it was the beginning of my ending my personal scarcity—my Groundhog Day! I disagreed with reality and began taking responsibility for my self-created situation by changing my inner world to one of affluence, not scarcity.

Your imagination—one of God's gifts to you; in fact, a gift that might be the Cosmic Intelligence itself—has that ability to create *any* reality in your inner world. In fact, this *is* the nuts and bolts of the Law of Attraction and must be done before *anything* manifests into objective reality. Imagine every day and night charging like an unstoppable rhino toward your desire and achieving it. It must be your predominant thought and belief, and any counter-thought to that predominant thought must be nuked immediately (thought substitution)!

Exercise #1: Undesired Reality: "You're broke!" Therefore, you must have a corresponding cause to that effect, like "I have trouble with earning money," or something similar. Simply change that cause (Be) to something like "I am wealthy" or "Money effortlessly flows to me"— involving the actual desired effect (Have)—then finish steps #3, 4, and 5 as directed.

Exercise #2: Desired Reality:

Note: This process is basically the same except for steps #1 and 2.

1. Write down every desired reality (goal), starting from the most urgent and then biggest to smallest.

2. Restate each goal as a goal redefined, meaning a completed reality.

3. Pick the most urgent desire needing to be manifested and imagine it completed in your inner world. Imagine this desire completed before retiring, upon awakening, and daily as is needed through repetitive thought, spoken word, and/or even a recording of your own voice stating this goal redefined as a completed statement. Note: If you make a recording in your own voice, I suggest falling asleep listening to it with earphones on.

Record it multiple times for at least an hour. This hour of work will be well-spent, as you'll be able to use it repeatedly every night, planting this desire into your subconscious mind.

4.   Upon any pushback from your mind or others, negative counter-thoughts, apply the Law of Substitution as described earlier.

5.   Give advance gratitude as if it has already been achieved by you! Suggestion: Make a recording in your own voice repetitively thanking the *Invisible Architect* in advance for manifesting this desire! This recording should be thirty to sixty minutes long. In it, be grateful for your desire achieved and how wonderful your life is in every aspect. Use your imagination. Then, with headphones on, listen to the recording in bed as you fall asleep. You'll be able to use it repeatedly every night, planting this desire already fulfilled into your subconscious mind.

Remember…once you convince your subconscious of this desire achieved, that's when the fireworks begin—only then!

Exercise #3: Goals Redefined (Achieved)

To change a goal to a completed inner reality, which is the first step to manifesting a completed outer reality, you must take time out of the equation. The reason is that having a goal is nice—better than not having a goal—but that still says, "I have not yet achieved something but want or hope to in the future." This is not a good instruction to get the *Invisible Architect* busy manifesting. Stating the goal as already achieved activates the *Invisible Architect* to get busy reorganizing the Intelligent Energy Field, where everything already exists as potential energy, into your desire fulfilled (manifested).

Whatever Is to Be Must Have Already Been!

1.   State your goal.
2.   Redefine your goal as a statement (affirmation) in present time.

Note: Once step #2 is completed, pick which goal you want to move forward on and start the "desired reality" exercise.

You can apply this exercise to any desire, big or small.

Examples:

Goal: "I am [desire]; I am!" (Declaration)

- **To be healthy:** I am healthy; I am!
- **To be debt-free:** I am debt-free; I am!
- **To earn 120k a year at your sales job:** I earn 120k a year at my sales job; I do!
- **To win a Grammy for your next CD:** I won a Grammy for my next CD; I have!
- **To repair your relationship with your daughter:** My daughter and I are doing great; we are!
- **To cure your long-term insomnia:** I effortlessly fall asleep; I do!
- **To be a successful NFL football player:** I am a successful NFL football player; I am!
- **To be happily married with a great family:** I am happily married with a great family; I am!
- **To have a great-paying job that you love:** I have a great-paying job I that love; I do!

Note: These are just short examples; you can, of course, be more detailed!

Example:

Goal: To have a great-paying job that you love, pays 120k+ a year, provides great benefits, and allows you to work from your home office so you can have more time freedom with your family and personal hobbies.

Goal Redefined:

- **Stated desire:** I have a great-paying job that I love, pays 120k+ a year, provides great benefits, and allows me to work from my home office so I can have more time freedom with my family and personal hobbies.
- **Declaration:** I most definitely do; thank you, *Invisible Architect.* You're the best!

Exercise #4: Gratitude

Now Gratitude: The natural gratitude you feel and express after something good happens in your life. The sequence is the achievement of a desire followed by a natural expression of gratitude!

Advance Gratitude: Reverse sequence, in that the event has not happened, yet you are being instructed to express gratitude, which initially makes no sense. Why would you give thanks before your desire was achieved? But it does make sense if you understand the theory of universes, that is...

Advance gratitude is not an expression of thanks for the event having been fulfilled in the Physical Universe; it is an expression of gratitude for the event having been imagined and achieved in your personal universe! Big difference! (See Cognition VI: The Different Universes.)

As mentioned earlier, if you want to efficiently employ the *Invisible Architect* to help you design your lifestyle, you must make a clear statement of your goal in the present, have 100 percent faith and feeling that it will be manifested, and express your thanks in advance of its corroboration in the Physical Universe.

Why? My theory is that the physics of the Quantum Intelligent Energy Field, where all energy and frequencies *already* exist, only reorganizes its energy into your desire when your WORD is clear and 100 percent believed by you, the observer creator of the desire. It doesn't respond effectively otherwise.

Example: A building architect would not even begin construction on a home without a clear professional blueprint. That's apparently the nature of the spiritual mechanics at play here, too. If the *Invisible Architect* created *all*, I sincerely doubt this *all* was created from anything less than a clear, thought-out, detailed postulate (blueprint) that had 100 percent certainty, love, and gratitude behind it. I mean, look at the magnitude and detailed design of the Universe. I mean, are you kidding?

Similarly, when we apply the Be-Do-Have sequence, our desire must be similarly executed as the WORD!

Now Gratitude Exercise:

Make a list of everything in your life that you are thankful for. This could be anything small or big and might take you awhile—days, weeks, or ongoing. Don't take anything for granted.

Examples: Be thankful for your health, job, home, family, talents, money in the bank, friends, religion, parents for bringing you into the world, yearly vacation, learning from your mistakes, sunshine, water to drink, pets, education, cell phone, books, neighbors, waking up each morning, breathing easily…You get the idea.

Remember, these examples of thanks have already manifested in your outer world. You are simply giving thanks for them in your life, which is very natural to do:

- I'm grateful that at my age, my body is generally in good health; thank you!
- I'm so grateful that my daughter got a scholarship, which has helped me with her college tuition.
- I'm so grateful my car is now paid off. Feels fantastic. Thanks!
- I'm truly grateful and humbled that my song "Good to Go" just went to number one on the Billboard jazz chart. Wow, unbelievable! Thanks!
- I'm excited my girlfriend has agreed to marry me!
- Thank you, God, for my new dream job as a journalist at WSEE-TV!
- I'm so thankful my mom's operation was a success!

Tip: You could make a recording on your cell and then play it back before retiring or during the day, especially if you're feeling down. Hearing these thanks back in your own voice will do wonders for raising your emotional frequency.

A grateful life leads to happiness and peace. Remember the Law of Substitution, which states no two thoughts can be occupying your mind at the same time. While you are being grateful, you can't be worrying, stressing, upset, jealous, angry, unhappy, etc. The more grateful you are, the closer you are to the frequency and energy of the *Invisible Architect*.

Gratitude is a like a key that unlocks the door of our heart. It helps us feel happy, whole, enriched, and confident. Instead of focusing on the things that are wrong, we focus on the things that are right.

Gratitude is like medicine that dissolves our inner disharmony instantly and for the moment brings us back to our deep spiritual connection with what is good and beautiful.

A grateful mind is a great mind that eventually attracts to itself great things!

Advance Gratitude Exercise:

Remember, these given examples of thanks have not yet manifested in your outer world. They are desires you have declared manifested in your personal universe but that you are thanking the Intelligent Energy Field in advance for fulfilling in the manifest or Physical Universe. Note: You are also thanking yourself in advance for all your activity and contributions to this imminent manifestation—you are not a passive, lazy spectator!

This first advance gratitude thank-you of mine, one of many, occurred *before* the real one above did, namely...

"I'm truly grateful and humbled that my song "Good to Go" just went number one on the Billboard jazz chart. Wow, unbelievable. Thanks!"

This is the advance gratitude thank-you that I started giving thanks to in September 2018 after I wrote the song "Good to Go." At that time, I declared it number one! I then imagined it number one every night before retiring and upon awakening; I felt all the emotions that I knew I would feel when it happened, and I graciously thanked in advance the *Invisible Architect* for making it so! I even went so far as to get a copy of the Billboard jazz chart and with Photoshop, altered the date and put my song and name at the number one slot! I looked at the altered chart every day until my subconscious accepted it as real. I did this consistently from September 2018 until mid-April 2019 when I got word that it shot up the charts to number one! I was only a few weeks off in the real world, but since I achieved number one a few weeks earlier, I held off reprimanding the *Invisible Architect* for being a few weeks late (Smile)!

I think you got the idea. Simply take one of your goals and rewrite in the present as a goal redefined—a statement of the desire already achieved. Be as creative as possible with the details, using your God-given imagination that can create anything instantly. Then give thanks repetitively as an added tool to assist the *Invisible Architect* in carrying out your desire.

Write as many of these thankful statements as you have goals redefined as completed desires. You can work on one at a time or all at once; do whatever works for your work ethic and attention span.

Your desire or idea is the substance of things hoped for and the evidence of things not seen. This is a great definition of faith. Your desire is as real as your heart pumping blood through your body.

It has its own frequency, shape, form, and substance in the Quantum Energy Field.

It is awaiting your declaration, your WORD! Regard this desire as a spiritual reality. Then, trust the Law of Growth and the *Invisible Architect* to make it so in the manifest reality.

Your WORD makes you the God of your universe, but to manifest it in the denser Physical Universe, you need to employ the *Invisible Architect*.

The *Invisible Architect* is ALL energy awaiting manifestation through the individual, and the individual can manifest only through the Universal.

If you haven't figured this out yet…You and the *Invisible Architect* are ONE!

The Connection is the Secret!

Mental action depends upon consciousness (being aware) of the power. Therefore, the more conscious you become of your unity with the source of all power, the greater your power will be to control and master any condition. Mental action is the interaction of the individual upon the Universal Mind, and as we established earlier, the Universal Mind is the intelligence that pervades all space and animates all living things. This mental action and reaction make up the Law of Causation and are how one manifests anything!

Exercise #5: Awareness of the *Invisible Architect*

"Everything that's created comes out of silence. Your thoughts emerge from the nothingness of silence. Your words come out of this void. Your very essence emerged from emptiness. All creativity requires some stillness." —Wayne Dyer

To employ the *Invisible Architect* to manifest our God-given desires, we must first establish the communication channel. Next, we must demonstrate to ourselves that the *Invisible Architect* does indeed exist and is part of our Divine nature and available to each of us if we understand the spiritual mechanics of it all.

We enter the Silence to consciously experience our oneness with the *Invisible Architect*. To do so, we must change the focus of our minds; we must withdraw our attention from the "noisy" manifest realm of effects and turn inward into the Silence of our inner world, where we seek and find the cause of all things, the Architect (God) as Spirit. God's presence in all its fullness is always available to us, for it is in, around, and through us. So, by going into the Silence and concentrating, we can make the *connection* between the finite and the Infinite, the limited and the unlimited, the visible and the invisible, the personal and the impersonal. Truthfully, we are always connected, but given the normal survival challenges, we are not naturally attuned to the God-Frequency to give and receive communications. Hence the need to shut down the conscious mind and go into the Silence to pray and meditate.

Remember, prayer is when you talk to God; meditation is when you listen to God.

Process:

1. First, go into a place free from distractions and make yourself comfortable.

2. Then do some deep breathing until relaxed. When you are comfortable and relaxed, the process of detaching from a normal state of consciousness can begin. It is therefore important to take the time needed to prepare the environment, body, and consciousness for entering the Silence.

3. Once you have disengaged from your everyday consciousness, close your eyes if you haven't already and concentrate on the God-frequency of love.

4. Now focus your thoughts (attention) on the phrases "I am," "I am love," "God is love," "God is within me," "God fills and surrounds me with his Divine presence," etc. By focusing on these concepts, we enter the intuitive faculty of our minds and discover there our link with God: "The secret place of the highest." This is the place in our consciousness where the *Invisible Architect* becomes visible to our perceptions and can be directly experienced, where believing becomes knowing, and where the God-frequency within becomes a personal reality. It's where we accomplish our connection with the all-loving Power within.

5. Imagine carrying this presence inside you and not being aware of it. (That would be analogous to not knowing you were a multimillionaire and therefore operating like you were poor!) Look and you shall see! Listen and you shall hear! Feel and you

will be overwhelmed with happiness and joy! And by the way, you'll know the experience when you become aware; trust me. So, have patience!

Whatever technique you use, the purpose is the same: to lead you into the secret place, a state of consciousness where we commune with the Intelligent Energy that created all things and will create your desires by expressing itself through you.

Since Be is the first step of existence, let alone manifestation, go into the Silence and know (become conscious or aware) that you ARE! This is just *being* and *perceiving*!

Everything is Energy; God is Love; Love is THE Energy!

The more you give and receive love, the closer you Be-come to the Intelligent Energy Consciousness, where everything already exists awaiting your observation and manifestation.

The only evidence I have personally of the existence of these spiritual mechanics is subjective and empirical in nature. You can prove it to yourself just as well through the same process of observation and experience.

So, go into the Silence and with eyes closed, repeat "I am love!"

Love is the *Invisible Architect*'s energy signature. Make it your signature, and all manner of good things (Bes, Dos, and Haves) will begin flowing into your life proportionate to your ability to be on this God-Frequency!

You are now ready to manifest anything!

You are what you will to be, and if you are being love—the energy signature of the *Invisible Architect*—everything is possible accordingly.

Exercise #6: Self-Discipline

So, what does self-discipline have to do with understanding and employing spiritual mechanics in our daily lives?

Everything!

It takes daily practice and self-discipline to a) become aware of the *Invisible Architect*, b) learn how to consciously commune with and use this wonderful intelligent energy, and c) have patience and trust it to manifest your desires as only it knows how to do!

Most of us are so busy with the challenges of modern-day survival that we have no time to devote to spiritual mechanics, which is a shame. There is more to life than just surviving—sleeping, going to work, paying bills, surfing the internet, posting on social media, watching TV, pampering our bodies, and beginning again the next day and the next, etc. We need to work smarter, not harder!

This is like the movie *Groundhog Day* I mentioned earlier. To break out of this self-created non-optimum life situation, one must posit a new cause and, through the Law of Cause and Effect and employment of the *Invisible Architect*, create a better, more optimum life situation.

To do that, it takes some effort, some elbow grease focused on the study and application of spiritual mechanics—our relationship between the Universal Consciousness and its creations and the interactions thereof. There is a lot of practical knowledge in this book and many others. But knowledge is useless if not applied repeatedly until it becomes second nature. And here is what's interesting about my last statement, as I reflect on what I just said: Isn't it odd that we have to study and practice these mechanics until we own them when in fact it is our nature as children of God to Be, Do, and Have what we desire?

How ironic that we have lost our way, which is a topic worthy of research. Technology is advancing by leaps and bounds, but spiritual growth, ethics, and work discipline are sorely lagging.

The first step is to get organized and disciplined at managing your time. Here's one of my favorite time management exercises:

1. Take inventory of *everything* you do for one week, and I mean everything, and be as detailed as possible.
2. Then, schedule your day the night before for one week.
3. Compare your intended schedule with what you really did.

4. Continue until you become master—causative—over your schedule.

Taking inventory of everything you do for a week is quite revealing! Once you see what you are actually doing, you'll be ready to reorganize and change things with a little self-discipline.

Example:

Time	Activity	Completed on Time?	
7 AM	Up, shower, breakfast	Yes	
8 AM	Travel to work	Yes	
9 to 12:00 Noon	Work job	Yes	
12 to 1 PM	Lunch, errands, etc.	Yes	
1 to 5 PM	Work job	Yes	
5 to 6 PM	Travel home	No	Home at 6:20 - Traffic
6:00 to 8 PM	Dinner, family time	Yes	
8 to 9 PM	Relax, TV, etc.	Yes	
9 to 10 PM	Work on book	No	Too tired…
11:00 to 7 AM	Bed	Yes but…	Restless night!

This exercise can do wonders for your time management and self-discipline and help you achieve your goals.

Story: I used to have a piano student who always said he didn't have time to practice, so he, of course, wasn't progressing very well. I told him one doesn't *have* time; one *creates* time, which was completely foreign to him. So, I told him to do step #1: the inventory assignment. I told him when he came for his next lesson to bring me an accurate inventory of everything he did to the minute. For example, going to bed, getting up; taking care of personal hygiene; traveling to work; working; eating lunch; commuting home; spending time with his family; watching TV;

exercising; spending time on his phone, internet, social media, etc.—everything!

What he discovered startled him, as he realized that he spent fourteen hours a week on social media and internet surfing, twelve hours watching TV, two hours on the phone, forty hours at his job, fifty-six hours sleeping, twelve hours commuting, three hours exercising, ten hours on personal hygiene, and nineteen hours feeding his body.

Now, there are 168 hours in a week. I didn't really need to point anything out to him, as he easily saw that even though he said learning the piano was important to him, his actions showed otherwise—twenty-six hours a week were being devoted to social media, internet, and TV. He then clearly saw that instead of making excuses about having no time to practice, he could easily practice two hours a day if he spent less time on social media and TV.[49]

He then went on to steps #2, 3, and 4 until he mastered his time.

Time, according to physicist Carlo Rovelli, is a mental process happening in the space between memory and anticipation. It is a collective act of introspection, narrative, record-keeping, and expectation that's based on our relationship to prior events and the sense that happenings are impending.

What I take away from this statement is time is arbitrary. It's not how much time you have; it's who you choose to Be and what you choose to Do in a certain *interval of time* that creates what you will Have. We therefore don't have time; we create time!

There's a lot of truth then to the maxim:

"If you want something done, give it to a busy person!"

—Benjamin Franklin

---

[49]NFL QB Kirk Cousins, who at the time of this writing earns 28 million a year, still uses a color-coded spread sheet in fifteen-minute increments to efficiently manage his time. He says it reduces the amount of mental energy he expends during the weekly grind and forces him to focus on what's important while eliminating time-consuming distractions.

Lifetime Perspective

Note: These are estimates and not applicable to everybody, depending on your lifetime, goals, and activities.

Table 1: Eighty-Year Lifespan, Basic Categories

Lifespan	80 years	29,200 days	700,800 hours
Sleep	26 years	9,733 days	233,600 hours
Awake	54 years	19,466 days	467,200 hours

Table 2: Other Categories

Work	20 years	7,580 days	182,000 hours
Worry	6 years	2,210 days	50,960 hours
Food	7 years	2,600 days	66,500 hours
TV, phone, internet, etc.	5 years	1,950 days	46,000 hours
Personal hygiene	4 years	1,516 days	36,400 hours
Free time	12 years	4,380 days	105,120 hours

As an exercise…

1. Look and reflect on Table 1 as to how many years, days, and hours on average you spend on some of these main categories.
2. Next, determine every category *you* are active in and calculate the time spent.
3. Finally, see if you can make some changes in these activities so they align more optimally to you achieving your desires.

Exercise #7: Mental Reboot Analogy

Computer: an electronic device for storing and processing data, typically in binary form, according to instructions given to it in a variable program.

- **Hardware:** the mechanical, magnetic, electronic, and electrical devices comprising a computer system, such as the CPU, disk drives, keyboard, and screen.
- **Software:** the instructions, usually written in binary code, that tell the computer what to do.

Software can be thought of as the variable part of a computer and hardware the invariable part.

Human Being: Spirit, mind, body; a being that possesses a body to inhabit with an interface called the mind to control the body to achieve various desires.

If a computer's hardware is intact—its motherboard, hard drive, keyboard, screen, etc.—but it's not functioning correctly or performing up to par, then there's probably a bug in the software. The software needs to be rebooted (turned off and restarted), its corrupt code fixed or updated, or both. Or just get a new one if it's unrepairable!

Regarding humans, if the body's intact, but you're not achieving your desires, then the spirit/mind (software) needs a reboot and/or debug... hence, the study and application of the spiritual mechanics covered in these shared Cognitions.[50]

Mental Reboot Exercises

1. Create a new software program and install it in your hardware! This translates to you reprogramming the old software—all old beliefs (fixed ideas) of scarcity, etc.—and in their place installing updated software that will serve your purpose. You do this by repetitively inputting new beliefs of abundance through positive affirmations until your new software is up and running and

---

[50] Depending upon your beliefs, you could order and pick up a new body via death and reincarnation and start anew if that is your belief and wish, but that would be a royal pain in the butt and only a last resort or when it's time!

creating new neural pathways of abundance to employ the *Invisible Architect*. You therefore have the ability of consciously creating your new mindset and making this happen.[51]

2. Now using the Law of Correspondence (your inner world creates your outer world) that we discussed in an earlier Cognition, do the following assignment daily to update your internal software and do a mental reboot.

   a. Write down every non-optimum outer world situation, starting from biggest to smallest.
   b. Determine the exact optimum situation for each non-optimum situation.
   c. State it as an affirmation or postulate as a completed reality in present reality—think it, say it out loud, record, listen, etc.
   d. Input it into your inner world through daily repetitive thought, spoken word, and/or even recording.
   e. Finally, give thanks for it already having been achieved—advance gratitude.

Note: During your daily activities, whenever one of your negative contrary-to-your-ideal fixed ideas or beliefs enters your mental space, replace the negative thought as soon as possible with its opposite positive twin. This is particularly important so as to not undo your mental reboot process.

Exercise #8: Law of Opposites

It's important to understand the following phenomena that can occur during the manifestation process:

1. Your failures contain the seeds of success.
2. Your success contains the seeds of failure.

---

[51]Suggested reading: *Consciously Creating Circumstances* by George Winslow Plummer

3. It is, however, your choice!

In *Conversations with God*, a book I highly recommend, Neale Donald Walsch describes how he had asked God some questions, but there were never any answers forthcoming. But then one day, he got an answer from God, which is the genus of his book. One of God's answers stated the opposite of everything we could ever wish to know or experience exists somewhere in the Intelligent Energy Field that our soul is connected to. Now, what does this mean? It means we might experience (attract) this opposite energy anytime during the manifestation process. Our soul sometimes does this to produce a context within which we might experience what it is that we desire. For example, what is tall without short, bad without good, lack without abundance, etc.?

This phenomenon, known as the Law of Opposites, states that the moment you state any desire, everything unlike your desire may begin manifesting! So, the next time something unwelcome occurs in your life, welcome it. Embrace it and bless it! Do not resist or condemn it. *What you resist persists.* Surrender to the process of creation—the Law of Opposites—and know that life itself is creating for you a perfect context for perfection itself to be experienced in, as, and through you.

Affirm—state the desire as fulfilled in the present—and then let go and believe in your heart it is on its way to you by special delivery!

If you begin experiencing any pushback or apparent failure, use that as a sign that the Quantum Intelligent Field has received your declaration (the WORD) and is in the middle of rearranging its energy, an energy where everything including your desire already exists, into your wish fulfilled. By creating order in your mental universe, disorder may temporarily show itself in the form of doubt, uncertainty, pushback, etc. Have you ever decided to clean out and rearrange a dirty closet? In the process you get dirty, bit by a spider, cut yourself, question why you decided to do this, and want to quit! The solution is to keep your original stated desire—a clean, organized closet—in play until it manifests, right?

So, smile and continue to allow the process to evolve into your ideal (the Law of Growth). The *Invisible Architect* may have to make many changes in your life, some very drastic, to manifest your desire. The manifestation process is dynamic and ongoing. If you prematurely evaluate changes as failure, you may interrupt this on-going process.

Sidebar story: I was earning good money with several sources of income but had a goal to make a lifestyle change with my music career. I stated my desire and did the Be-Do-Have Law of Cause and Effect exercise, and all hell broke loose in my life. I very quickly lost two good sources of income and almost interfered with the manifestation process, as it *appeared* to be going the wrong way. I was puzzled, but I bit my tongue, hung in there, and embraced what life was throwing at me, and lo and behold, the *Invisible Architect* was simply rearranging my Quantum Energy Field in a radical way. This had to be done to prepare my consciousness and my garden to grow my new desire. The result was my number one song "Good to Go" on the Billboard jazz chart. Had I panicked and been impatient, I might have dug up my desire-seed prematurely and sabotaged the *Invisible Architect*'s work in progress.

Remember, real conscious manifesting begins with your belief about your desire. When you have faith in yourself, then there is a congruency between the universal energy and your energy, a vibrational alignment. And it is this alignment that works to fulfill all your desires through the Be-Do-Have process.

"The best way out is always through."

—Robert Frost

If you put your attention on the opposite unwanted reality that you may be experiencing as pushback, you will slow and potentially even stop the manifestation process due to your counter-energy. And yes, your thoughts, beliefs, and attitudes are that powerful because they are wired to the *Invisible Architect*, who is always acting upon them—especially your predominant ones!

And please don't ask me why, as I don't know! It apparently was set up this way, which I find fascinating, as it allows for total self-determinism, which is very loving and refreshing—what a miracle, this thing called life!

Exercise #9: Mindset/Stress Exercises

Thought is a form of energy. Focused thought possesses the innate ability to influence, restructure, and ultimately mold the energy in the Quantum Intelligent Field.

The less dense the energy environment, the faster the restructuring may occur. (Notice the difference in ease and speed of manifestation between the thought and Physical Universe.)

Proposed Axiom:

The effectiveness and speed that thought takes to restructure an energy environment is determined by the intensity, clarity, and consistency of the thought and the density of the energy environment upon which it is acting.

Therefore, don't make thoughts or statements that you don't want to manifest! And don't agree with external statements from others, books, news, etc., that if agreed with could create an undesirable reality. If you do, have patience; embrace what's happening and simply substitute a positive thought in its place, as discussed earlier. This is thought substitution.

Why? Because all thoughts/statements, whether from within or from without, if agreed with and continued, especially if predominant, lead to more of the same. Thoughts lead to beliefs, beliefs lead to decisions, and decisions lead to actions and changed realities! If you're going to change your outer reality, then change it into something desirable…make sense?

THOUGHTS CREATE REALITY, WHETHER YOU BELIEVE IT OR NOT!

Be-Do-Have
Thought-Action-Reality
Strategy-Execution-Success
Inner World Creates Outer World

Below are eight different statements, from negative to positive, that postulate different mindsets:

1. I won't do it.
2. I can't do it.
3. I want to do it.
4. How do I do it?
5. I'll try to do it.
6. I can do it.
7. I will do it.
8. Yes, I did it; it's done!

Exercise:

Locate your mindset awareness characteristic on this scale regarding any desire or non-optimum situation you wish to manifest or change, be it as simple as reorganizing your office or as complicated as patching up a relationship, losing weight, earning six figures a year, paying for a vacation, winning a gold medal, eliminating stress, whatever. If it's not a 6, 7, or at best an 8…you have some mindset issues to handle ASAP, as anything lower than a 6 will not serve you very well. If you want the *Invisible Architect* 100 percent on your team, you'll need to be clearly at an 8!

Affirm every day, "Yes, I did it; it's done" to your desire(s) or situations(s) and then give thanks (advance gratitude) for it having already been achieved, even though in physical reality, it hasn't yet. Happy manifesting!

This is vital!

Exercise #10: The Joy of Giving!

"For it is in giving that we receive."—Saint Francis of Assisi

"The sole meaning of life is to serve humanity."—Leo Tolstoy

"We make a living by what we get; we make a life by what we give."—Winston Churchill

"If you want happiness for an hour, take a nap. If you want happiness for a day, go fishing. If you want happiness for a year, inherit a fortune. If you want happiness for a lifetime, help somebody."—Chinese proverb

The Emotional/Spiritual Side of Giving

Buddha said that no true spiritual life is possible without a generous heart. Generosity allies itself with an inner feeling of abundance—the feeling that we have enough to share. As we discussed earlier, the God-Frequency is love. Giving is the outward expression of love, especially when the giver expects nothing in return. This is true unconditional love! When you give unconditionally, you are matching the *Invisible Architect*'s frequency—the God-Frequency where everything exists awaiting the WORD—with your desire fulfilled.

The Science Side of Giving

The science behind giving is a little more complicated, but I was surprised to discover there is indeed some correlation with the spiritual side. There is a deeper current to giving than just feeling good. In 2006, Moll and Jordan Grafman, neuroscientists at the National Institutes of Health, scanned the brains of volunteers as they were asked to think about a scenario involving either donating a sum of money to charity or keeping it for themselves. Their results demonstrated that when the volunteers placed the interests of others before their own, the generosity activated a primitive part of the brain that usually lights up in response to food or sex. Donating (giving) affects two brain "reward" systems working together: the midbrain ventral tegmental area[52](VTA), which also is stimulated by food, sex, drugs, and money; as well as the subgenual area, which is stimulated when humans see babies and romantic partners.

The exchange we get in the case of giving is the "warm glow"—the positive emotional feeling we get from helping others. Moll said that their 2006 study "strongly supports the existence of 'warm glow' at a biological level. It helps convince people that doing good can make them feel good; altruism therefore doesn't need to be only sacrifice."

Their experiment provided the first evidence that the "joy of giving" has a biological basis in the brain—it is hard-wired in the brain and pleasurable.

The idea of altruism behaving like a miracle drug has been around for at least two decades. The euphoric feeling that we experience when we help others is what researchers call the "helper's high," a term first introduced twenty years ago by volunteerism and wellness expert Allan Luks to explain the powerful physical sensation associated with helping others. As Harvard cardiologist Herbert Benson puts it: "Helping others is a door through which one can go to forget oneself and experience our natural hard-wired physical sensation."

In other words, the helper's high is a classic example of nature's built-in reward system for those who help others.

So, how great is that?

----

[52]"The ventral tegmentum area is a group of neurons located close to the midline on the floor of the midbrain. The VTA is the origin of the dopaminergic cell bodies of the mesocorticolimbic dopamine system and other dopamine pathways; it is widely implicated in the drug and natural reward circuitry of the brain. The VTA plays an important role in a number of processes, including reward cognition (motivational salience, associative learning, and positively valenced emotions) and orgasm, among others, as well as several psychiatric disorders." Wikipedia, the free encyclopedia

When we give unconditionally, we not only raise our frequency closer to the God-Frequency, where anything can be manifested, but also receive an emotional spiritual high and a physical dopamine high at the same time!

As Mahatma Gandhi said, "To find yourself, lose yourself in the service of others."

If you always give, you will always have. To give is to receive. The miracle of giving is that it comes back to you in greater abundance than you could ever give.

But what if you're not rich? Say you don't have lots of money to give to charities, family, friends, causes, etc.

First, be careful of that dangerous affirmation, "I'm not rich; I don't have lots of money…" That's a clear goal redefined into a statement of reality, and you'd better replace it with its opposite ASAP, or the Intelligent Energy will get to work on making and keeping that non-optimum condition (effect) a reality, which you don't want!

If you're not rich in money, you still can still serve.

You can give love, support, validation, humor, assistance, kindness, yourself, thanks, a gift, a get-well card, money, your time, food, encouragement, old clothes to Salvation Army, help to a stranger, blood, a smile, your skills, etc.…

"It's not how much we give but how much love we put in the giving."
—Mother Teresa

"No one is useless in this world who lightens the burden of another." — Charles Dickens

The rewards of giving are priceless. If you want to have happiness, you need to give happiness. If you want love, you need to give love. If you want money, try giving some away. It is only in giving that you receive.

No matter what your circumstances in life, you always can give something, always.

Look for opportunities where you can give and help others. The gift of joy will come to you when you give of yourself to others.

Practice giving something every day. Make it a habit. It could be something as simple as letting an elderly person in front of you in line at the bank. Or helping somebody lift their carry-on to the baggage compartment. Or paying it forward at Starbucks by paying for the person's drink behind you.

But be careful how much you give. If you give too much, you may receive too much and become way too happy—then what? You'll have to create depression to keep your newfound happiness in context!

In other words, per the Law of Opposites, the universe just may decide for you to experience unhappiness for a while, so you'll appreciate happiness more next time around!

Exercise #11: Relaxation Breathing

According to Health Harvard Publishing, the term "fight or flight" is also known as the stress response. It's what the body does as it prepares to confront or avoid danger. When appropriately invoked, the stress response helps us rise to many challenges. But trouble starts when this response is constantly provoked by less momentous, day-to-day events, such as money woes, traffic jams, job worries, or relationship problems.

Health problems are one result. A prime example is high blood pressure, a major risk factor for heart disease. The stress response also suppresses the immune system, increasing susceptibility to colds and other illnesses. Moreover, the buildup of stress can contribute to anxiety and depression. That said, we can develop healthier ways of responding to them.

As discussed in **Cognition 12**, there is a big difference between being proactive about a situation and finding a solution versus unnecessary destructive worry and stress, which does nothing to solve the problem and, if anything, makes it worse. When the mind is engaged in stress, worry, or fear—negative emotions—it's impossible to be happy, excited, enthusiastic, inspired, or anything else, and therefore you won't be effective at achieving much of anything.

There are three solutions to stress. Each of these move you from being part of the effect (victimized) to being part of the cause (proactive).

1. Drop what you're doing and focus in real time on handling the situation causing the stress. Example: The roof is leaking; don't worry about it—get it fixed!
2. If that is not possible for various reasons, then "park" the problem in some way for future handling and get on with your current activity. This takes disciplined control of unwanted thoughts and possibly some planning. Example: It's Friday, and you just got a letter from the IRS that you are being audited. You initially freak out, and your mind starts imagining all kinds of disasters, right? Wouldn't it be better to just park this until Monday when you can meet with your tax accountant and come up with a plan? Of course!
3. Use thought substitution, which states that the mind cannot hold two thoughts simultaneously. Therefore, substitute any positive thought in place of the unwanted thought that's causing the stress hormone release. Although any positive thoughts will do, it would be much better to kill two birds with one stone and immediately apply the Be-Do-Have process of the Law of Cause and Effect formula. Namely, state the problem as solved (Be), then imagine your life with this problem solved along with all the feelings and emotions you'd be experiencing (Do) and express advance gratitude for the problem solved and wish fulfilled (Have). Are you getting the modus operandi yet?

But before you choose any of these solutions, it is important to collect your dispersed thought energy. Any mental or physical task demands concentration, which could be defined as focused thought energy. If, for example, driving a car safely demands 150 units of thought energy but you only have 95, as the rest are unavailable and stuck in a worrisome problem, then your driving is at risk. It would be better to not get behind the wheel until you're able to collect enough units of thought energy (attention)for the task at hand. Many accidents could be avoided if this was done.

There are many types of controlled breathing techniques to help you collect your dispersed thought energy, but I have found this diaphragmatic/visualization highly effective to do anywhere:

1. Sit up comfortably in a chair or lie back on a flat surface, like your bed, with your head supported.
2. Take in a deep breath slowly through your nose so your stomach moves up and out for about four seconds (diaphragmatic breath). While inhaling, think "I am mentally calm and physically relaxed," "I am calm and relaxed," "I am harmonious," "I am stress-free," or any such phrase.
3. Lift and tighten your stomach muscles at the top of the breath and hold your breath for a few seconds—four to six seconds, whichever is comfortable.
4. Put your tongue lightly up on your front palate (roof of your mouth) so you can easily control (slow down) your exhale breath. Note: Letting it out all at once may only take a couple of seconds, which is not what you want.
5. As you exhale through your mouth, let your tightened abdominal muscles relax and exhale slowly, making your breath last at least eight seconds, which is easy to do with your tongue controlling your exhale breath. While exhaling, state to the universe, "I am!" which is your declaration of your previous inhale statement in step #2 ("I am harmonious, I am!").
6. Continue the process and take deep breaths in and out, feeling your stomach rise in on inhalation and out on exhalation. Do this until you feel physically and mentally relaxed. Sometimes it only takes a few minutes to achieve relaxation and alleviate stress.

Deep breathing improves blood flow, decreases blood pressure, increases energy level, reduces inflammation, detoxifies the body, stimulates the lymphatic system, and helps collect your dispersed thought energy units, which are needed in life to perform any mental or physical task.

Exercise #12: Daily Personal Success Affirmations

Repeat the following personal affirmations daily upon retiring and upon awakening and anytime you feel your mindset going negative. They should be stated repeatedly with the feeling and gratitude you would have if they have already been achieved.

These declarations, your WORD, done right, can literally redesign your life! Remember, what you're doing is contacting and employing the power of the *Invisible Architect*. These are not just useless statements if done with feeling and faith.

Personal Success Affirmations

I am who I am.
I am what I will be.
I am always loving.
I am harmonious.
I am perfect.
Everything I desire is within me.
I have everything I need.
I am happy.
I am strong.
I am healthy.
I am wealthy.
I am complete.
I am powerful.
I easily express the perfection within me.
I am a miracle of creation.
Life is a miracle.

I shed my life of lack and scarcity and am grateful for my life of abundance.

I am one with the *Invisible Architect*; the *Invisible Architect* is one with me.

I serve others effortlessly and willingly.

I am not alone; I always employ the *Invisible Architect* to manifest all of my Divine desires.

ACKNOWLEDGEMENTS

The conception of *The Invisible Architect* came about directly from the recognition of an "inner voice" as mentioned in Cognition 2, when I received the following order:

"John, you now need to spread the WORD!"

I first want to thank the *Invisible Architect* for expressing itself through me. Thank you!

I also want to thank myself for paying attention to this life-changing miracle, inviting it into my life, and following its advice. I can't imagine missing this opportunity!

I would also like to thank and mention the following people and sources for their research, writings, quotes, and inspiration:

J. S. Bach, Joseph Murphy, Neville Goddard, Scott Alexander, Dr. Joe Dispenza, Eckhart Tolle, Ernest Holmes, Thomas Troward, William Buhlman, Deepak Chopra, Jane Roberts, Charles Haanel, Carlo Rovelli, Florence Scovel Shinn, Carl Sagan, Marcus Aurelius, Ernest Hemingway, Dalai Lama, Ralph Waldo Emerson, Franz Kafka, Neale Donald Walsch, Henry Ford, Wallace D. Wattles, George Winslow Plummer, W. Clement Stone, Napoleon Hill, Jim Rohn, the Beatles, the Bible, Jesus, Jorge Moll & Jordan Grafman, Tania Kotos, Robin Sharma, Mark Twain, Zig Ziglar, Albert Einstein, Alphonse Karr, Lao Tzu, Hans Christian Andersen, and Harvard Health Publishing.

And a very special thanks to Mark Januszweski and the Master Key Mastermind Alliance. The *Invisible Architect* very covertly led me to Mark through a network marketing business I was working with my wife on the side. I was surfing the Internet for network marketing training for my distribution team and came across Mark J, "The World's Laziest Networker!" Mark is an internationally acclaimed "trainer's trainer," as far as network marketing goes. Mark built six network marketing empires from the ground up and then paid it forward with his Go90Grow "boot camp" for network marketers. Although network marketing led me to Mark, I soon saw the promotion for his world-renowned self-discovery course Master Key Master Mind Alliance (MKMMA) and realized that was the real reason I was led to him (smile)! Mark's passion is helping people understand that the wealth they seek already lies within them. I was already a student of spiritual growth, and my inner voice said I should hook up with Mark, so I did. My sincere thanks to Mark J, as he is sometimes referred to, for helping me polish my Divine purpose!

And an incredible special thanks to my wife, Barbara Novello, for contacting me after thirty-eight years and folding her life into mine and for her never-ending love and support, without which this endeavor would have been quite lonely and difficult, if not impossible.

And finally, I can't thank the *Invisible Architect* enough for not only sending my first girlfriend and soulmate back to me but for literally saving her from the 911 disaster that I spoke about in Cognition 2. If that is not a demonstration of the existence of the power and love in each of us, then I don't know what is!

Your perfect life awaits your decision to claim it!

ENDNOTES

Why This Book?

1. Neville Goddard: "I of myself can do nothing, the Father within me He doeth the work."
2. Charles Haanel: "Life is that quality or principle of the Universal Energy which manifests in so-called organic objects as growth and voluntary activity, and which is usually co-existent in some degree, with some manifestation of that same Universal Energy as the quality or principle termed intelligence."
3. Ralph Waldo Emerson: "Once you make a decision, the universe conspires to make it happen."

Cognition 1

1. Siddhartha Gautama: "Watch your thoughts; they become words. Watch your words; they become actions. Watch your actions; they become habits. Watch your habits; they become your character. Watch your character; they become your destiny."
2. Charles Haanel, *Mental Chemistry*: "Mental action is the interaction of the individual upon the Universal Mind, and as the Universal Mind is the intelligence which pervades all space and animates all living things, this mental action and reaction is the Law of Causation."

Cognition 2

1. Lao Tzu: "At the center of your being, you have the answer; you know who you are, and you know what you want."
2. Joseph Murphy: "He must consciously commune with the Indwelling Power and Presence, and receive guidance, strength, vitality, and all things necessary for the fulfillment of his needs."

Cognition 3

1. Ernest Holmes, *The Science of the Mind*: "Perfect life within me, come forth into existence through me of that which I am and lead me ever into the paths of perfection causing me to see only the good; and by this process, the soul shall be illumined, acquainted with God and shall be at peace."

2. James Redfield: "We have been disconnected from the larger source of dynamic universal energy that sustains us and responds to our expectations. We have cut ourselves off and so have felt weak, insecure and lacking."

3. Charles Haanel: "It only requires recognition to set causes in motion which will bring about results in accordance with your desire, and this is accomplished because the Universal can act only through the individual, and the individual can act only through the Universal; they are one."

Cognition 4

1. Dr. Joe Dispenza, *Becoming Supernatural*: "There is an invisible field of energy and information that exists beyond this three-dimensional realm of space and time—and that we have access to it."

2. William Walter Atkinson: "Mind in itself is believed to be a subtle form of static energy, from which arises the activities called 'thought,' which is the dynamic phase of mind. Mind is static energy; thought is dynamic energy—the two phases of the same thing."

3. Charles Haanel, *The Master Key System*: "To control circumstances a knowledge of certain scientific principles of mind-action is required."

4. Bob Proctor "The space around us is not empty. It is full of a living essence, which is like a conduit that carries our mental frequencies out into the field of possibility."

Cognition 5

1. Zig Ziglar "You have to Be before you can Do and Do before you can Have."

2. Dr Joseph Murphy *To Be, To Do & To Have*.

3. Theodore Roosevelt: "Nobody cares how much you know, until they know how much you care."

4. Florence Scovel Shinn: "There is a Divine Design for each person, something that you are to do which no one else can do. There is a perfect picture of this in your higher self or God mind and usually flashes across your consciousness as an unobtainable ideal."

5. Joseph Murphy, *The Miracle Power of Your Mind*: "Desire, according to the pioneer of success thinking Joseph Murphy, is behind all progress. It is the push of the Life-Principle. It is an Angel of God telling us

something which, if accepted by us, will make our life fuller and happier."

6. Charles Haanel: "If you use electricity for light, you call it good. If you grasp a wire which has not been properly insulated and it kills you, it is not for that reason bad or evil. You were simply careless or ignorant of the laws governing electricity. For the same reason, the one Infinite Power, which is the source of all Power, manifests in your life either as good or as evil, as you make use of it constructively or destructively."

7. Neville Goddard, *The Power of Imagination*: "Only Love knows love and love knows only love."

Cognition 6

1. Thomas Troward, *The Hidden Power*: "I am the Person that thou art, and thou art the Person that I am."

2. Matthew 21:22: "And all things, whatsoever ye shall ask in prayer, believing, ye shall receive."

Cognition 7

1. Carl Sagan: "The cosmos is within us. We are made of star-stuff. We are a way for the universe to know itself."

2. Dalai Lama: "In our quest for happiness and the avoidance of suffering, we are all fundamentally the same, and therefore equal. Despite the characteristics that differentiate us—race, language, religion, gender, wealth and many others—we are all equal in terms of our basic humanity."

3. Ralph Waldo Emerson: "Every particular in nature, a leaf, a drop, a crystal, a moment of time is related to the whole, and partakes of the perfection of the whole."

4. Neville Goddard, *The Power of Imagination*: "An assumption—whether conscious or unconscious—builds a bridge of incidences that lead inevitably to the fulfillment of itself."

5. John Wheeler, scientist-philosopher who introduced the concept of wormholes and coined the term "black hole"(1911–2008), postulated we live in a "participatory universe," which emerges from the interplay of consciousness and physical reality, the subjective and objective realms. He pioneered the theory of nuclear fission with Niels Bohr and introduced the S-matrix (the scattering matrix used in quantum mechanics). Wheeler devised a concept of quantum foam: a theory of "virtual particles" popping in and out of existence in space. Similarly,

he conceptualized foam as the foundation of the fabric of the universe.

6. Charles Haanel, *The Master Key System,* 1912: "There is a world within— a world of thought and feeling and power; of light and life and beauty and, although invisible, its forces are mighty." "The world within is governed by mind. When we discover this world, we shall find the solution for every problem, the cause for every effect; and since the world within is subject to our control, all laws of power and possession are also within our control." "The world without reflects the world within. What appears without is what has been found within. In the world within may be found infinite Wisdom, infinite Power, infinite Supply of all that is necessary, waiting for unfoldment, development and expression. If we recognize these potentialities in the world within, they will take form in the world without." "The world without reflects the circumstances and conditions of our consciousness within."

7. Lennon and McCartney, "I Am the Walrus": "I am he as you are he as you are me and we are all together."

8. Anna Serphimidou Vayaki: "Exception: Particles have spins. Particles that have integer spin are called bosons and can occupy the same space at the same time, meaning the probability of finding one in an (x,y,z) coordinate increases the more of them there are. Bosons can occupy the same quantum state in general. Particles with half integer spin are fermions and follow the fermi-dirac statistics, and thus cannot occupy the same space; i.e., the probability of finding one in an (x,y,z) spot will always be the probability for finding one particle; only one can occupy a quantum state at a time, in general."

9. James Lake, MD, of Stanford University: "extensive research has confirmed the medical and mental benefits of meditation, mindfulness training, yoga, and other mind-body practices."

Cognition 8

1. Joseph Murphy: "Disciplined or controlled imagination is one of the primal faculties of mind and has the power to project and clothe your ideas, giving them visibility of the screen of space."

2. Franz Kafka: "By believing passionately in something that still does not exist (faith), we create it. The nonexistent is whatever we have not sufficiently desired."

3. Robert Collier, *Secrets to Spiritual Abundance*: "Having gratitude for something before you receive it is the secret catalyst to Spiritual manifesting."

4. Ernest Holmes, *The Science of Mind*: "God is Word, God is Law, God is Spirit. The Word of God means the power of spirit to declare Itself into manifestation. The starting point of all creation is the WORD. The Word is the Concept, Idea, Image, or thought. God, the Architect, speaks and it is done!"

5. John 1:1: "In the beginning was the Word, and the Word was with God, and the Word was God."

6. Dr Joe Dispenza, *Becoming Supernatural*: "The key is remembering the future."

Cognition 9

1. Cornerstone Christian Ministries: "Prayer—the world's greatest wireless connection."

2. W. Clement Stone: "Prayer is man's greatest power."

3. *The Tibetan Book of the Dead*, Bardo Thodol by Padmasambhava, also known as Guru Rinpoche.

4. *The Egyptian Book of the Dead*, developed from a tradition of funerary manuscripts dating back to the Egyptian Old Kingdom. Its chapters and spells were first written down on papyrus around 1600 BC. Translated in 1842 by German Egyptologist Karl Richard Lepsius.

5. Mark Januszewski, "The Master Key Experience": The Master Key Mastermind Experience is a twenty-six-week course on self-discovery and self-achievement https://masterkeyexperience.com/about/

6. The Bible (from Koine Greek τὰ βιβλία, tà biblía, "the books") is a collection of sacred texts or scriptures. The Bible is the inspired Word of God and relates how the Creator expresses his undying love for his creation of mankind. Varying parts of the Bible are considered to be a product of Divine inspiration and a record of the relationship between God and humans. The main authors are Moses, John, Paul, and other disciples over a period of time.

7. George Anderson, *We Don't Die*.

8. William Buhlman, *Adventures in the Afterlife*.

9. Robert Bruce, *Astral Dynamics: The Complete Book of Out of Body Experiences*.

10. John 14:13: "And whatsoever you shall ask in my name, that will I do."

Cognition 10

1. Jim Rohn: "Success is neither magical nor mysterious. Success is the natural consequence of consistently applying basic fundamentals."
2. Charles Haanel, *The Master Key System,* 1912: "The only way by which we may secure possession of power is to become conscious of power, and we can never become conscious of power until we learn that all power is from within."
3. Thomas Troward, *The Dore Lectures*: "The Divine ideal (desire) can only be externalized in our objective life in proportion as it is first formed in our thought. And it takes form in our thought only to the extent to which we apprehend its existence in the Divine Mind. By the nature of the relation between the universal mind and the individual mind, it is strictly a case of reflection; and in proportion as the mirror."
4. Tania Kotsos, "Brain Waves and the Deeper States of Consciousness." www.mind-your-reality.com/brain_waves.html
5. Ernest Holmes, *The Science of Mind*: "Where your mind goes, energy flows."

Cognition 11

1. Charles Haanel: "Behind every effect there is a cause, and if we follow the trail to its starting point, we shall find the creative principle out of which it grew. Proofs of this are now so complete that this truth is generally accepted."
2. Gordana Biernat: "What you think you Become. Your thoughts create you. What you DO you ARE. Your actions define you."

Cognition 12

1. Ernest Holmes, *The Science of Mind*: "Where your mind goes, energy flows."
2. Eckhart Tolle: "Everything that exists has being, has God-essence, has some degree of consciousness. Consciousness is the light emanating from the eternal Source. Being, consciousness and life are synonymous."
3. Dr Wayne Dyer: "I am that I am"—These are the words written in the spiritual literature of the Torah, also called the Pentateuch—the first five books of the Old Testament in which God tells Moses this is my name forever, a name by which I shall be known for all future generations "I Am That I am."

https://www.youtube.com/watch?v=A96OI4b8sFY

4. George Matthew Adams: "Learn to keep the door shut, keep out of your mind and out of your world every element that seeks admittance with no definite helpful end in view."

Cognition 13

1. Ralph Waldo Emerson: "For every minute you remain angry, you give up sixty seconds of peace of mind."
2. Robin Sharma: "Forgiveness isn't approving what happened. It's choosing to rise above it."
3. Mark Twain: "Forgiveness is the fragrance that the violet sheds on the heel that has crushed it."
4. Zig Ziglar: "Gratitude is the healthiest of all human emotions. The more you express gratitude for what you have, the more likely you will have even more to express gratitude for."
5. Albert Einstein: "There are only two ways to live your life. One is as though nothing is a miracle. The other is as though everything is a miracle."
6. Alphonse Karr: "Some people grumble that roses have thorns; I am grateful that thorns have roses."
7. Lao Tzu: "Being deeply loved by someone gives you strength, while loving someone deeply gives you courage."
8. Marcus Aurelius: "When you arise in the morning, think of what a precious privilege it is to be alive—to breathe, to think, to enjoy, to love."
9. Unknown Author: "We make a living by what we get, but we make a life by what we give."
10. Desmond Tutu: "Hope is the ability to see that there is light despite all of the darkness."
11. Charles Haddon Spurgeon: "Faith goes up the stairs that love has built and looks out the windows which hope has opened."
12. Siddhartha Buddha: "No true spiritual life is possible without a generous heart."
13. 1 Corinthians 13:4-5: "Love is patient, love is kind. It does not envy, it does not boast, it is not proud. It does not dishonor others, it is not self-seeking, it is not easily angered, it keeps no record of wrongs."
14. Lennon and McCartney, "I Am the Walrus": "I am he as you are he as you are me and we are all together."
15. Og Mandino, *The Greatest Salesman in the World*: "This too shall pass."

Cognition 14

1.   Ernest Hemingway: "There is nothing noble in being superior to your fellow man; true nobility is being superior to your former self."
2.   Norman Mailer: "Every moment of one's existence, one is growing into more or retreating into less."
3.   Ernest Holmes: "Perfect life within me, come forth into expression through me of that which I am and lead me ever into the paths of perfection causing me to see only the good; and by this process, the soul shall be illumined, acquainted with God and shall be at peace."

Cognition 15

1.   Robin Sharma: "There are no mistakes in life, only lessons. There is no such thing as a negative experience, only opportunities to grow, learn and advance along the road of self-mastery."
2.   John Powell: "The only real mistake is the one from which we learn nothing."
3.   Emerson: "Every calamity is a spur and a valuable hint."
4.   Neville Goddard, *The Power of Imagination*: "Thinking from the end."

Cognition 16

1.   Ralph Waldo Emerson: "All I have seen teaches me to trust the creator for all I have not seen."
2.   William James: "The greatest discovery of any generation is that a human can alter his life by altering his attitude."

Cognition 17

1.   Hans Christian Andersen: "Every man's life is a fairy tale written by God's fingers."

Author's Commentary (Epilogue)

1.   Isaac Bashevis Singer: "Life is God's novel. Let him write it."

Addendum 1

1. Henry Ford: "Whether you think you can, or you think you can't—you're right."
2. John 1:1: "In the beginning was the Word, and the Word was with God, and the Word was God."
3. Wallace D. Wattles, *The Science of Getting Rich*: "The man who owns all he wants for the living of all the life he is capable of living is rich; and no man who has not plenty of money can have all he wants and needs."

Addendum 2

1. Albert Einstein: "There are only two ways to live your life. One is as though nothing is a miracle. The other is as though everything is a miracle."
2. Napoleon Hill: "There is one quality which one must possess to win, and that is definiteness of purpose, the knowledge of what one wants, and a burning desire to possess it."
3. Scott Alexander, *Rhinoceros Success*.
4. Wayne Dyer: "Everything that's created comes out of silence. Your thoughts emerge from the nothingness of silence. Your words come out of this void. Your very essence emerged from emptiness. All creativity requires some stillness."
5. George Winslow Plummer, *Consciously Creating Circumstances*.
6. Neale Donald Walsch, *Conversations with God*.
7. Robert Frost: "The best way out is always through."
8. Saint Francis of Assisi: "For it is in giving that we receive."
9. Leo Tolstoy: "The sole meaning of life is to serve humanity."
10. Winston Churchill "We make a living by what we get; we make a life by what we give."
11. Chinese proverb: "If you want happiness for an hour, take a nap. If you want happiness for a day, go fishing. If you want happiness for a year, inherit a fortune. If you want happiness for a lifetime, help somebody."
12. Mother Teresa: "It's not how much we give but how much love we put in the giving."
13. Charles Dickens: "No one is useless in this world who lightens the burden of another."

INDEX

A

Absolute Spirit, 34
advance gratitude, 72–76, 103, 111, 131
  conscious energy field, 72
  exercise, 205–6
  mental time travel, 76
  Word is Spiritual Law, 73
Adventures in the Afterlife (Buhlman), 83
advice, by inner voice
  business advice, 14, 21–22
  career advice, 9–12, 18–19
  medical advice, 12
  networking advice, 15
  on death, 12–13
  on life, 13
  on playing goals, 10, 16–17
  to solve financial crisis, 10
affirmations, 109, 123, 185–93
  "to be" statements, 185–88
  goals redefined, 189–90
  money, 190–91
  personal success, 226–27
  powerful, 188–89
after-death communications (ADCs), 82
Alexander, Scott, 198
Andersen, Hans Christian, 179
Astral Dynamics: The Complete Book of Out of Body Experiences (Bruce), 83
Atikinson, William Walker, 33
Aurelius, Marcus, 142
awake states, 106
awareness, of Invisible Architect, 207–9

B

Bach, Johann Sebastian, 43, 96
Be-Do-Have formula, 131, 132, 142, 185, 196
Be-Do-Have-Sequence, 69–77, 97, 102, 41–46
  car analogy, 107
  designing lives, 44–46
  desire and, 41
  execution, 42
  Law of Attraction, 41
  life is for lessons, 165
  love and, 43
  manifestation process, 70
  spiritual marksmanship, 128–37
beingness of divinity, 43
Benson, Herbert, 221
bosons, 63
brain wave frequencies, 98–100
Bruce, Robert, 83
Buhlman, William, 83
business advice, by inner voice, 14, 21–22

C

car analogy, 107
career advice, inner voice on, 9, 11, 18–19
  and encouragement, 9
Celestine Prophecy, The (Redfield), 25, 169, 170
Chinese bamboo tree, story of, 173–75
Collective Intelligence, 99
Collier, Robert, 72
connection, secret, 207–9, 207–9

life is for lessons, 161–66
  Be-Do-Have-Sequence, 165
  belief on, 162
  chronic non-optimum situations in
    life, 163
  Law of Thought Substitution, 163
life's purpose, 94–95
love, 43, 44, 145–47, 193, 209

M

Mailer, Norman, 153
Manifest Universe, 53
manifestation
  corroboration by, 72
  outer-world, 163
  process, 70, 105
Manifester, 35
Master Key System(Haanel), 42
mechanics, definition of, 25
mental action, 175, 207
mental reboot analogy, 213–15
mental thieves, 124
mindset or stress exercises, 218–19
miracle, 143
  forgiveness, 143–44
  giving, 144–45
  gratitude, 147–48
  hope, 148–49
  loving, 145–47
money affirmations, 189, 190–91
money antibiothics, 191–92
money antibiotics, 190
Mother Teresa, 222
Murphy, Joseph, 7, 42, 69
music career, inner voice on, 9

N

nature of reality, inner voice on, 9, 15
networking advice, inner voice on, 15

nirvana, 105
now gratitude, 72, 103, 203
  exercise, 204–5

O

opposite negative unwanted reality,
  108
ordering intelligence, 3–4
  intelligent, 29
outer reality, 201
out-of-body experiences and
  techniques (OBEs), 15, 82, 83

P

participatory anthropic principle
  (PAP), 59
Particular Spirit, 34
Pauli Exclusion Principle, 121
Perfect All-Knowing Power, 26
perfect omniscient energy, 50
personal growth and development,
  153–57
  personal dreams and, 154
  self-improvement, 153
  spiritual growth, 154
personal success affirmations, 226–27
Personal Thought Universe, 87
Personal Universe, 53
physical collective reality, 63
Physical Universe, 36, 45, 53, 72, 87,
  120, 131, 199
  building in, 93–94
  dense lower-frequency, 186, 187
  desire in, 89
  frequency and density of, 89
  sequence of thoughts, 62–65
  vs. personal thought universe, 63
Platinum Hit (song), 15
positive thinking. *See also* affirmations

ABOUT THE AUTHOR

John Novello is an internationally acclaimed jazz pianist and composer who has performed with many well-known groups as well as leading his own groups Niacin and the John Novello Band. He has had several top ten hits on the Billboard Jazz Chart, one of them, "Good to Go" reaching number one. In addition to John's musical accomplishments, John is an author & music educator, having written the best-seller industry keyboard method *The Contemporary Keyboardist,* published by Hal Leonard. John resides in Franklin, TN with his wife, Barbara Novello.

Follow John at:

keysnovello.com
www.linkedin.com/in/john-novello-421231/
Instagram.com/keysnovello
facebook.com/john.novello.3
Twitter.com/keysnovello

john@keysnovello.com

CPSIA information can be obtained
at www.ICGtesting.com
Printed in the USA
JSHW032054120123
36081JS00001B/1

9 781647 192198